San Antonio CUISINE

San Antonio CUISINE

A Sampling of Restaurants & Their Recipes

Compiled and Edited by

KAREN HARAM

Two Lane Press

ISBN 1-878686-11-9

Printed in the United States of America

Cover design, hand lettering, and text ornaments: Calvert Guthrie
Editing and text design: Jane Doyle Guthrie
Food consultant: Judith Fertig
Map: Leigh Melton Singleton

10 9 8 7 6 5 4 3 2 1   94 95 96 97 98

Two Lane Press, Inc.
4245 Walnut Street
Kansas City, MO 64111
(816) 531-3119

Lovingly dedicated to my husband, Mark; my daughters, Jennifer and Emily; and, my mother, Gertrude Wolfe.

◪ Contents

◤ Acknowledgments

Without the generosity of San Antonio restaurateurs and chefs, there could have been no *San Antonio Cuisine*. I thank them for their willingness to put aside pressing restaurant demands to get me recipes, as well as for sharing my enthusiasm for the project.

Gratitude goes to my husband, Mark, whose help with this book was invaluable. Besides being my most loyal taster—toting leftover test recipes with him to work for lunch each day for a year—he handled kitchen cleanup, no small task when the testing of approximately 225 recipes is involved. His support and love are never ending, and I am grateful.

Thanks go to my daughters, Jennifer and Emily, who learned to forgo dining on their favorite home recipes in lieu of whatever recipe I needed to test. Their help with typing and correspondence is greatly appreciated as well.

Loyal friends Robin Hudnall and Carol Boudreaux generously helped test recipes. Whit Boudreaux offered assistance as well, as did my supper club companions, Lenny and John Angel, Judy and Richard Smith, and Nora and David Williams. Thanks also go to Judyth Rigler, *San Antonio Express-News* book editor, and my sister, Nancy Ginzel, who offered encouragement as well as assistance.

The *San Antonio Express-News* was enthusiastic about my participation in *San Antonio Cuisine*. I appreciate their constant support, not just of my involvement with this book, but with any project I take on.

A special thanks to Karen Adler, who asked me to be a part of *San Antonio Cuisine* and encouraged me throughout the project; to Judith Fertig and editor Jane Doyle Guthrie, for their editing skill; and to Shifra Stein, for her assistance.

⚡ Introduction

Thanks to the wealth of tourists who visit San Antonio each year and learn about its food firsthand, the Alamo City is known nationwide for its restaurants. Sizzling fajitas, tortilla soup, barbecue, Gulf Coast seafood, and margaritas are just a few of the specialties for which San Antonio is famous.

On their own, the city's signature foods are a delight. Served in an ambience of fun and festivity for which San Antonio is acclaimed, in settings ranging from the River Walk to the Texas Hill Country, the food takes on a special flavor not soon forgotten.

San Antonio is best known for its Tex-Mex and Southwestern specialties. After all, this is the area that introduced chili, fajitas, and breakfast tacos to the rest of the country. But there's more to San Antonio food than just the best enchilada plate to be found in the United States—there's Italian and Mediterranean, Vietnamese and Thai, Spanish and German, French and Continental, not to mention Cajun, country, and Southern.

The city's restaurateurs are not only inventive in executing memorable recipes, they're generous in passing along the results of their labors. Restaurant owners and chefs were gracious in sharing their best recipes for *San Antonio Cuisine*, in many cases adapting them so they could be prepared by home cooks. Most of the ingredients called for in their recipes are readily available in supermarkets, although a few may require a trip to a specialty market. Plus, all the recipes in *San Antonio Cuisine* have been home tested to ensure they can be easily duplicated in your own kitchen.

The recipes selected for inclusion in *San Antonio Cuisine* were chosen not only for their flavor, but for their ease of preparation. With few exceptions, these recipes are simple to prepare and rely on flavorful, fresh ingredients, not lengthy ingredient lists, for their superb taste.

When someone finds out that I have what I consider the best job in South Texas—that of food editor of the *San Antonio Express-News*—the first question I'm usually asked is, "What's the best restaurant in San Antonio?" I've yet to respond to that question with a definitive answer. I truthfully say that there is no "best restaurant" in San Antonio, but there are lots of best restaurant dishes.

Lots of those best dishes, from the top restaurants in San Antonio, are included in the following pages. Enjoy them, and the flavor of San Antonio, as you sample the best of *San Antonio Cuisine*.

Karen Haram

Beginnings

☎ Asparagus-Citrus Salad

3/4 pound fresh asparagus, cleaned and tough stems removed
1/4 cup extra-virgin olive oil
1/4 cup fresh orange juice
Salt and pepper to taste
1 medium orange, peeled, seeded, and sectioned

Cook asparagus in boiling water until barely tender. Mix olive oil and orange juice with salt and pepper to make a dressing.

Divide asparagus among 4 chilled plates and place 2 orange segments across the spears. Spoon dressing over salad and serve.

The asparagus, oranges, and dressing in this zesty, fresh-tasting salad can be prepared ahead of serving time and assembled at the last minute.

Serves 4

LUIGI'S RESTAURANT
6825 San Pedro
San Antonio, Texas 78216
(210) 349-5251

☎ Cascabel Crispy Noodle Salad with Ancho-Lime Dressing

1/2 package wonton skins
3–4 cups vegetable oil
3/4 (8-ounce) package rice sticks (available at Asian markets)
1 (10-ounce) bag fresh spinach, stemmed, cleaned, and shredded
1 yellow bell pepper, seeded and slivered
1 red bell pepper, seeded and slivered
1/2 cup sliced almonds, toasted
1/4 cup fresh basil leaves, julienned
1/4 cup fresh mint leaves, julienned

Cut wonton skins into 1/4-inch strips. Heat oil until hot. Fry wonton strips in small batches. Drain on paper bags or paper towels and set aside. Also in small batches, fry rice noodles in hot oil (noodles will puff up quickly when added to hot oil; remove immediately). Drain well and set aside.

Place remaining ingredients in a large bowl. Shake **Ancho-Lime Dressing**, add to salad, and toss. Gently fold in fried wontons and rice sticks.

Cold cooked wild rice also can be tossed with this salad, if desired. Either way, it wins raves.

Serves 8

Ancho-Lime Dressing

1-1/2 tablespoons grated lime zest
4-1/2 tablespoons fresh lime juice
3 tablespoons firmly packed brown sugar
1 tablespoon minced fresh ginger
6 tablespoons finely minced green onions
3/4 teaspoon freshly grated nutmeg
3 tablespoons honey
4-1/2 tablespoons finely julienned ancho chili (soften chili in hot water for 2 minutes, remove seeds, and roll like a cigar to julienne)
3/4 teaspoon Tabasco sauce
3/4 teaspoon soy sauce
3/4 teaspoon balsamic vinegar
1-1/2 tablespoons extra-virgin olive oil

In a nonmetallic bowl, combine all ingredients except oil. Slowly add oil and whisk well.

This dressing can be made ahead and stored up to 2 weeks, refrigerated.

Makes about 1 cup

CASCABEL RESTAURANT
Sheraton Fiesta Hotel
37 Northeast Loop 410
San Antonio, Texas 78216
(210) 366-2424

☖ Barley and Papaya Salad

1 (16-ounce) box barley
1 medium red bell pepper
1 medium poblano chili
3 medium ears fresh corn, husked
3 papayas, peeled, seeded, and diced
1/4 cup minced cilantro
Juice of 1 large lime
3 tablespoons champagne vinegar
1/2 cup plus 2 tablespoons extra-virgin olive oil
Salt and freshly ground pepper to taste

Wash barley in cold water several times. Transfer to a pan with 3 quarts of salted water and bring to a boil, then reduce heat to a simmer and cook until tender, about 30 minutes (do not overcook). Drain barley and rinse well with cold water, then refrigerate to chill.

Halve red pepper and poblano chili, remove seeds, and core. Place peppers on a grill with corn and roast for 7 minutes. Dice peppers and add to barley. With a knife, slice kernels from corncobs and add to barley. Add remaining ingredients and toss gently. Taste and adjust seasoning, if necessary, then refrigerate for at least 45 minutes before serving.

This can become a main course if you add 1-1/2 pounds of grilled or sautéed shelled shrimp to the salad.

Serves 12 to 14

CHAPS RESTAURANT/RIVER BEND SALOON
Hyatt Regency San Antonio
123 Losoya
San Antonio, Texas 78205
(210) 222-1234

⌂ Smokehouse Cranberry Salad

2 (3-ounce) packages cherry
   gelatin
2 cups boiling water
1 (16-ounce) can whole-berry
   cranberry sauce
1 (7-ounce) can crushed
   pineapple, drained well
1/4 cup finely minced celery
Mayonnaise and fresh
   cranberries

Dissolve gelatin in hot water, then let it cool slightly. Stir in cranberry sauce, drained pineapple, and celery, then pour mixture into a 6-cup mold or 8 to 10 individual gelatin molds. Chill overnight or until firm. Top each portion with a small dollop of mayonnaise and garnish with fresh cranberries, if desired.

This is excellent as a condiment with a sandwich or chicken and dumplings, or perfect with your Thanksgiving or Christmas turkey.

Serves 8 to 10

NEW BRAUNFELS SMOKEHOUSE
6450 North New Braunfels
San Antonio, Texas 78209
(210) 826-6008
140 Highway 46 South
New Braunfels, Texas 78130
(210) 625-2416

⌂ Marinated Sourdough Bread and White Bean Salad

4 ounces dry large white beans (preferably Scarlett Runner), rinsed and drained
1/4 pound sourdough bread, 2 to 3 days old
1-1/4 teaspoons salt
1/2 teaspoon freshly ground pepper
1/4 cup balsamic, sherry, or red wine vinegar
2 large (1-pound) vine-ripened tomatoes, cubed
1 large cucumber, peeled, seeded, and cubed
1 medium red onion, diced
2 tablespoons minced fresh basil
2 tablespoons minced fresh mint
1/4 cup plus 1 tablespoon extra-virgin olive oil
Arugula

Place cleaned beans into a saucepan with enough cold water to cover by 2 inches. Bring to a boil, then turn off heat and let beans set for 40 minutes. Return to heat and cook beans until just tender, about 30 minutes, adding additional hot water if needed (do not overcook). Drain and set aside to cool, reserving cooking water.

Preheat oven to 350 degrees. Cut bread into large cubes and arrange in a single layer on a baking sheet. Bake until lightly browned (about 8 to 10 minutes), tossing once. Remove from oven, cool, and transfer to a large bowl. Sprinkle with salt, pepper, and 2 tablespoons vinegar, and allow to marinate for 1 hour. Add beans with about 1/4 cup of cooking water to bread, followed by tomatoes, cucumbers, onion, and herbs. Drizzle with olive oil and remaining vinegar. Gently stir, then allow to marinate at room temperature for 1 hour.

Taste and adjust seasonings, if necessary, adding additional olive oil and vinegar if the salad is too dry. Serve at room temperature on arugula-lined plates. (If not serving immediately, refrigerate, then bring to room temperature before serving.)

It's important to use a firm-textured bread that is several days old so it stays firm and doesn't get soggy.

Serves 4

PAESANO'S
1715 McCullough
San Antonio, Texas 78212
(210) 226-9541

☎ Red Jacket Potatoes in Whole-Grain Mustard Vinaigrette with Marinated Tomatoes and Texas Goat Cheese

6 slices bacon, diced
1/4 cup olive oil
1 large yellow onion, diced
6 cloves garlic, minced
2 shallots, minced
6 tablespoons red wine vinegar
2 tablespoons balsamic vinegar
4 tablespoons whole-grain
  mustard
2 teaspoons chopped fresh
  basil
2 teaspoons stemmed and
  chopped fresh thyme
Freshly cracked pepper and
  kosher salt to taste
12 red potatoes, cooked,
  peeled, quartered, and
  sliced
8 ounces soft Texas goat
  cheese

Prepare **Marinated Tomatoes** and set aside.

Heat olive oil in a pan over medium heat. Add onion, garlic, and shallots. Sauté until translucent. Add bacon and cook until crisp, then deglaze pan with red wine vinegar. Remove pan from heat and add balsamic vinegar, mustard, basil, thyme, pepper, and salt. Gently fold in potatoes, then spread mixture in a large attractive baking dish. Spread **Marinated Tomatoes** on top of potato salad, then spread goat cheese on top of tomatoes. Place in oven under the broiler until cheese is lightly browned, and serve.

This full-flavored potato salad works well on a buffet table.

Serves 12

Marinated Tomatoes

6 Roma tomatoes, diced
2 cloves garlic, minced
1 shallot, minced
1 teaspoon dried thyme
1 teaspoon dried basil
2 tablespoons extra-virgin olive
  oil
2 tablespoons balsamic vinegar
Freshly cracked pepper and
  kosher salt to taste

Combine all ingredients in a medium nonmetallic bowl and allow to marinate at room temperature.

Makes about 2 cups

LAS CANARIAS
La Mansion del Rio Hotel
112 College Street
San Antonio, Texas 78205
(210) 225-2581

⌂ Pasta Salad with Roasted Peppers and Poultry

6 cups diced roasted duck, chicken, or turkey
1-1/2 cups extra virgin olive oil
4 red bell peppers
2 whole heads garlic
16 ounces tricolor rotini or ziti, cooked al dente
1 medium red onion, diced small
1/2 cup chopped hearts of palm
1 tablespoon chopped fresh basil
1 tablespoon chopped fresh parsley
2 tablespoons chopped fresh chives
1/4 cup (about 16) sliced kalamata olives (available at gourmet markets and many large groceries)
1/2 cup red wine vinegar
1/4 cup balsamic vinegar
1 teaspoon salt
1/2 teaspoon freshly ground pepper
Fresh greens, such as Boston lettuce, radicchio, or chopped Romaine

Preheat oven to 425 degrees. Dip fingers into olive oil and rub oil onto peppers and garlic until well coated. Arrange peppers and garlic on a baking sheet and roast until skins are nicely charred (about 45 minutes). Remove peppers and garlic and put into a bowl covered with foil. Let steam for about 10 minutes.

Peel peppers, remove seeds, and chop to a small dice. Cut the bottoms off of garlic heads and squeeze pulp onto diced peppers.

Warm remaining olive oil in a saucepan and add peppers and garlic. Remove pan from heat and add duck, chicken, or turkey. Stir in pasta and remaining ingredients except fresh greens. Taste and adjust seasonings, then mound salad onto plates lined with Boston lettuce, radicchio, chopped Romaine, or anything with lots of color.

This is good served cold at a summer picnic or warm on a cool fall evening (it's a perfect way to use leftover roasted turkey). Try it with a hot crusty bread as an accompaniment. If desired, the peppers and garlic in oil can be prepared up to 2 days in advance and refrigerated. The longer they set, the more flavorful the oil.

Serves 8

L'ETOILE
6106 Broadway
San Antonio, Texas 78209
(210) 826-4551

☙ Shrimp and White Bean Salad

1 pound medium shrimp,
  peeled and deveined
1/4 pound dry Great Northern
  white beans, rinsed and
  drained
1-1/4 teaspoons salt
2 tablespoons plus 2 teaspoons
  fresh lemon juice
1 bay leaf
1-1/2 cups diagonally sliced
  celery
1/2 cup (4 ounces) kalamata
  olives (available at gourmet
  markets and many large
  groceries)
1 medium red onion, diced
1 clove garlic, sliced very
  thinly
1/4 cup extra-virgin olive oil
1/4 teaspoon freshly ground
  black pepper
1 tablespoon minced fresh
  thyme (or 1 teaspoon dried)
1 tablespoon minced fresh
  oregano (or 1 teaspoon
  dried)
1 tablespoon minced fresh
  rosemary (or 1 teaspoon
  dried)

Place cleaned beans into a saucepan with enough cold water to cover by 2 inches. Bring to a boil, then turn off heat and let beans set for 40 minutes. Return to heat and cook beans until just tender (about 30 minutes), adding additional hot water if needed (do not overcook). Drain and set aside to cool, reserving cooking water.

Cook shrimp in boiling water until just done (about 1-1/2 minutes). Drain and transfer to a large bowl with salt, lemon juice, and bay leaf. Add warm beans to shrimp with about 1/4 cup of cooking water. Do not stir; let marinate at room temperature for 30 minutes.

Add remaining ingredients to mixture and allow to marinate at room temperature for 1 hour before serving. Taste and adjust seasonings, if necessary, adding additional vinegar and olive oil if mixture is too dry. (If not serving immediately, refrigerate, then bring to room temperature before serving.)

This robust salad is relatively low in calories but full of flavor.

Serves 4

PAESANO'S
1715 McCullough
San Antonio, Texas 78212
(210) 226-9541

☎ Wild Rice and Lump Crabmeat Salad

1 pound fresh Gulf lump
  crabmeat, picked well
1 (6-1/4-ounce) package Uncle
  Ben's Wild Rice Blend,
  cooked and cooled
1/2 red onion, finely diced
1/2 pound fresh mushrooms,
  thinly sliced
1 bunch fresh asparagus,
  washed, trimmed, and cut
  into pieces
1 (15-ounce) can garbanzo
  beans, rinsed and drained
1 to 1-1/4 cups Wishbone
  Creamy Italian Salad
  Dressing

Combine rice with onion, mushrooms, asparagus, beans, and salad dressing. Just before serving, gently toss in crabmeat and mix well with other ingredients.

This salad may be served on individual plates, stuffed into tomato or avocado halves, or used as a filling for a gourmet luncheon finger sandwich.

Serves 6 to 8

FIESTA TEXAS CATERING
17000 Interstate 10 West
San Antonio, Texas 78269
(210) 697-5164

☎ Chicken and Fresh Spinach Salad

1 pound boneless, skinless
  chicken breasts, cooked,
  cooled, and cubed
1 (10-ounce) bag fresh
  spinach, rinsed, steamed,
  and well drained
1/2 cup mayonnaise
2/3 teaspoon prepared
  mustard
Dash of Tabasco sauce
Salt and pepper to taste

Whirl spinach in a food processor or blender with mayonnaise, mustard, and Tabasco sauce. In a medium bowl, stir spinach mixture into chicken cubes and toss. Add salt and pepper to taste.

Serve this delicious salad as a sandwich filling or in tomato cups.

Serves 4 to 6

TWIN SISTERS BAKERY AND CAFE
6322 North New Braunfels
San Antonio, Texas 78209
(210) 822-2265

☎ Crosswalk Chicken Salad

1 whole chicken, boiled with 1
  chopped onion and 2
  chopped celery stalks,
  cooled
1/2 cup shredded red cabbage
1/2 cup chopped celery
1/2 cup sliced black olives
1/2 cup chopped red apple,
  with skin
Dried or minced fresh basil to
  taste
Freshly ground pepper to taste
Mrs. Dash to taste
Mayonnaise to taste

Debone chicken, discarding skin and bones. Tear or shred meat into strips. Place chicken in a large bowl and add cabbage, celery, olives, apple, basil, and spices. Stir in mayonnaise to desired moistness. Taste and adjust seasonings as necessary and serve.

This combination makes wonderful sandwiches. Or, use it to create pretty salad plates—place a scoop of chicken salad on a large green lettuce leaf, adding tomato wedges, a black olive, and alfalfa sprouts on the side, and sprinkling chopped walnuts over the top.

Serves 10 to 12

CROSSWALK DELI
121-C Alamo Plaza
San Antonio, Texas 78205
(210) 228-0880

♨ Smoked Turkey and Bacon Salad

8 thick slices bacon, cooked crisp and crumbled into small pieces (about 1 cup)
4 cups cubed smoked turkey
1-1/2 cups chopped celery
1/2 cup sweet pickle relish
1/2–1 cup homemade or good-quality commercial mayonnaise (no substitutes)

In a large bowl, gently toss together bacon, turkey, and celery. Add relish, followed by just enough mayonnaise to lightly coat mixture but not overpower taste.

This makes a delicious sandwich filling or stuffing for ripe tomatoes.

Serves 8

NEW BRAUNFELS SMOKEHOUSE
6450 North New Braunfels
San Antonio, Texas 78209
(210) 826-6008
140 Highway 46 South
New Braunfels, Texas 78130
(210) 625-2416

☎ Old-Fashioned Corn Bread Salad

1 (10-inch) skillet cooked corn bread
8–10 slices bacon, crisply fried and crumbled
2 large tomatoes, peeled and diced
2 bunches green onions, chopped (include part of green tops)
1 green bell pepper, chopped
1 red bell pepper, chopped
Salt and freshly ground pepper to taste
1 (17-ounce) can cream-style corn
1 tablespoon prepared mustard
1/2–3/4 cup mayonnaise (no substitutes)

Crumble corn bread into a large bowl, then add bacon and toss lightly. Add tomatoes, onions, bell peppers, salt, pepper, and corn. Stir in mustard. Add mayonnaise in small portions, being careful not to make mixture too soggy. Transfer salad to a large container with a tight-fitting lid and refrigerate for several hours.

Before serving, let stand at room temperature for about 30 minutes to bring out maximum flavor.

This is a great substitute for corn bread dressing during the holidays because it can be prepared up to a day in advance.

Serves 8

ARLENE'S CAFE
426 Seventh Street
Comfort, Texas 78013
(210) 995-3330

☎ Walnut Salad Dressing

2 green onions
6 sprigs fresh parsley
1/4 cup finely chopped walnuts
1-1/2 cups plus 2 tablespoons
  mayonnaise
6 tablespoons buttermilk
1-1/2 teaspoons minced fresh
  garlic
1 teaspoon salt
Scant 1/2 teaspoon white
  pepper
2 teaspoons paprika
Scant 1/2 teaspoon dried
  tarragon leaves
4 teaspoons sugar
1-1/2 tablespoons tarragon
  vinegar

Wash green onions and parsley and shake dry, then pat dry with paper towels. Chop 1/2 inch off the ends of green onions and discard. Whittle leaves off parsley. Chop onions and parsley leaves finely by hand, then combine with remaining ingredients and mix well. Refrigerate in a tightly covered container.

Serve this smooth, mellow dressing over mixed greens garnished with fresh tomatoes, alfalfa sprouts, and croutons.

Makes 2 cups

WATER STREET OYSTER BAR
999 East Basse, Suite 130
San Antonio, Texas 78209
(210) 829-4853

⌂ Honey Fruit Salad Dressing

2/3 cup sugar
1 teaspoon dry mustard
1 teaspoon paprika
1 teaspoon celery seed
1/4 teaspoon salt
5 tablespoons white vinegar
1 tablespoon fresh lemon juice
2/3 cup honey
1 teaspoon grated onion
1 cup vegetable oil

Whirl sugar, mustard, paprika, celery seed, and salt in a food processor or blender. Add remaining ingredients and blend until smooth.

Serve on the side as a dressing for fruit salad or as a dip for fruit on a buffet. This is a wonderful alternative to poppy seed dressing.

Makes about 2 cups

SUGAR-BAKER'S
5114 Broadway
San Antonio, Texas 78209
(210) 820-0306

♜ White French Salad Dressing

1 medium onion, quartered
1 small garlic clove
1 tablespoon fresh lime juice
1-1/8 teaspoons red wine
   vinegar
1/2 teaspoon salt
1/4 teaspoon white pepper
3–4 cups mayonnaise

In a food processor, puree onion and garlic together. Transfer to a bowl and add lime juice, vinegar, salt, and pepper, stirring well. Add enough mayonnaise to thicken. Whisk together until thoroughly blended, then refrigerate tightly covered.

This tangy dressing is delicious served over a salad of fresh greens, garden tomatoes, cucumbers, cheese, and croutons.

Makes 3 to 4 cups

GREY MOSS INN
19010 Scenic Loop Road
Helotes, Texas 78023
(210) 695-8301

☎ Twin Sisters Vegetable Soup

2 tomatoes, chopped
1/2 onion, chopped
1 large clove garlic, minced
1/2 tablespoon dried oregano
9 cups water
2 potatoes, cubed
2 yellow squash, cubed
2 zucchini, cubed
1 calabacita (a Mexican squash similar to zucchini), cubed
1 large carrot, peeled and cubed
1/2 stalk celery, cubed
1/2 green bell pepper, cubed
1/4 pound fresh green beans, cut into 1-1/2-inch pieces
1 cup (2 ears) fresh corn kernels
1 cup cooked red beans (rinse well if using canned)
Salt and freshly ground pepper to taste

In a large pot, simmer tomatoes, onions, garlic, and oregano in 1 cup water until onions are tender, about 15 minutes. Add remaining water and potatoes, squashes, carrot, celery, bell pepper, green beans, and corn. Cook until vegetables are tender, about 30 to 45 minutes, adding additional water if needed. Add red beans and cook for about 10 minutes more. Season well with salt and pepper, and serve.

This soup is very thick, like a stew. Add water to your personal preference, but don't let the mixture get too thin. This soup is also very low in fat.

Serves 8 to 10

TWIN SISTERS BAKERY AND CAFE
6322 North New Braunfels
San Antonio, Texas 78209
(210) 822-2265

☎ Gazpacho

1 (46-ounce) can tomato juice
1 (28-ounce) can whole
   tomatoes with liquid, diced
   finely
1/2 bunch green onions, sliced
   finely (tops included)
1 onion, diced finely
1/2 red bell pepper, diced
   finely
1 tablespoon finely diced
   jalapeño chilies
1/2 bunch cilantro, chopped
   finely
3 cucumbers, peeled, seeded,
   and grated
Juice of 2 lemons
1/4 cup red wine vinegar
2 tablespoons Maggi
   Seasoning (available at Asian
   markets)
Salt and pepper to taste

Combine all ingredients and refrigerate tightly covered for 24 hours before serving.

This zesty soup will keep in the refrigerator for 4 days.

Serves 12 to 14

BISTRO TIME
5137 Fredericksburg Road
San Antonio, Texas 78229
(210) 344-6626

☎ Chilled Fruit Soup

1/2 gallon pure unsweetened
   natural apple juice
1 cinnamon stick
2 tablespoons plus 1 teaspoon
   cornstarch
1/4 cup dry white wine
1/2 pint fresh raspberries,
   washed and picked
1/2 pint fresh blueberries,
   washed and picked
1 pint fresh strawberries,
   washed, hulled, and halved
1 fresh peach, washed, peeled,
   and diced finely
Fresh lemon twists (optional)
Mint leaves (optional)

In a large soup pot, bring apple juice to a boil with cinnamon stick. Boil for 10 minutes, then remove cinnamon stick and discard.

Mix cornstarch with white wine to make a smooth liquid. With apple juice boiling, pour cornstarch mixture into juice and whisk for 1 minute. Reduce heat and simmer for 20 minutes. Remove from heat, strain into a storage container, cool, and then refrigerate covered overnight.

To serve, arrange prepared fruit in 8 wide, flat bowls. Ladle approximately 1/2 cup chilled soup over fruit and top each bowl with a fresh lemon twist and a mint leaf, if desired.

This unusual cold soup is a wonderful change of pace from its warm, savory cousins. It can be served as an appetizer or as a dessert.

Serves 8

FIESTA TEXAS CATERING
17000 Interstate 10 West
San Antonio, Texas 78269
(210) 697-5164

♜ Santa Fe Corn Soup

3-1/2 cups (8–12 ears) fresh
  corn kernels or frozen corn
1 cup chicken broth
1/4 cup (1/2 stick) butter or
  margarine
2 cups milk (or 1 cup
  evaporated milk and 1 cup
  water)
1 garlic clove, minced
1 teaspoon dried oregano
  leaves
Salt and pepper to taste
3 tablespoons canned diced
  green chilies, rinsed
1 cup cubed cooked chicken
1 cup grated Monterey Jack
  cheese
1/4 teaspoon baking soda
1 cup diced fresh tomatoes
Fried tortilla triangles and
  fresh oregano

Combine corn and chicken broth in a blender or food processor and puree. Transfer to a 3-quart saucepan, combine with butter or margarine, and simmer slowly for 5 minutes, stirring to keep corn from sticking to bottom of pan. Add milk, garlic, oregano, salt, and pepper, and bring to a boil.

Reduce heat, stir in chilies and chicken, and simmer for 5 minutes. Remove from heat and add cheese and baking soda (to prevent curdling). Stir until cheese melts. To serve, ladle soup into 6 bowls, topped with diced tomatoes and garnished with tortilla triangles and a sprig of fresh oregano.

This corn soup recipe has all the flavors reminiscent of Santa Fe. Serve it with a pretty green salad and flour tortillas the next time you entertain.

Serves 6

THE PEACH TREE GIFT GALLERY AND TEA ROOM
210 South Adams Street
Fredericksburg, Texas 78624
(210) 997-9527

▲ Spinach Vichyssoise

5 ounces (1/2 of a 10-ounce bag) fresh spinach, rinsed and drained
2 medium potatoes, peeled, cooked, and diced
1-1/2 cups chicken stock
2/3 cup heavy cream
Salt and white pepper to taste

Parboil spinach for 1 minute and drain. Place spinach, potatoes, and half of chicken stock in a blender or food processor and puree. Add remaining ingredients and whirl for 30 seconds. Transfer to a covered container and chill for 2 hours before serving.

This easy, elegant soup is guaranteed to become a favorite. Be sure not to overseason; canned chicken broth can be salty.

Serves 4

CRUMPETS
5800 Broadway, Suite 302
San Antonio, Texas 78209
(210) 821-5600

▲ Elote y Poblano Soup

3–4 poblano chilies
1 medium white onion
1/4 cup corn oil
4 ears fresh corn
3 cups water
2 cups chicken broth
2 (12-ounce) cans evaporated
   milk
Salt to taste

Slice poblano chilies and onion, and sauté in oil for 10 to 15 minutes or until tender. Cut corn off cobs and boil kernels and cobs in water until corn is cooked and cooking liquid is flavored, about 30 minutes. Remove cobs from liquid and add chicken broth, evaporated milk, onion-poblano mixture, and salt. Let simmer for about 15 minutes (do not boil), then remove from heat and serve.

This corn and poblano chili soup reheats well and stays fresh in the refrigerator for several days.

Serves 8

LA CALESA
2103 East Hildebrand
San Antonio, Texas 78209
(210) 822-4475

▲ Jalapeño-Potato Soup

1 medium onion, chopped
1/4 cup (1/2 stick) butter or
    margarine
5 pounds russet potatoes,
    peeled and cubed
8 cups chicken broth
1 teaspoon ground cumin
1/4–1/2 cup coarsely chopped
    pickled jalapeño chilies and
    liquid
Pinch of baking soda
4 cups evaporated milk
Salt and pepper to taste
Sour cream and chopped
    green onions

In a large stockpot, sauté onion in butter or margarine until just tender. Add potatoes, chicken broth, and cumin, then cover and cook until potatoes are tender (about 20 to 30 minutes).

Remove from heat and add jalapeños, baking soda (to prevent curdling), and evaporated milk. Coarsely mash potatoes in the pot with a potato masher. Stir well, then season with salt and pepper. Return to heat and simmer for 15 minutes, stirring frequently. Garnish individual servings with a dollop of sour cream and a sprinkling of chopped green onions.

This is one of the owners' newest soup recipes and is fast becoming a favorite of their customers. In fact, Gourmet Magazine *requested this recipe!*

Serves 16 to 18

THE PEACH TREE GIFT GALLERY AND TEA ROOM
210 South Adams Street
Fredericksburg, Texas 78624
(210) 997-9527

⬛ Gini's Lentil Soup

1 pound (2 cups) dry lentils,
  rinsed and drained
8 cups water
1-1/4 pounds potatoes (about 2
  large), peeled and cubed
1 chopped onion
1/4 pound carrots (about 2
  medium), chopped
2 cloves garlic, minced (or 1/4
  teaspoon garlic powder)
1 tablespoon Maggi Seasoning
  (available at Asian markets)
1 bay leaf
Salt and pepper to taste

Place lentils and water in a large pot, add potatoes, and bring to a boil. Reduce heat and skim any foam off the top. Add onion, carrots, garlic, Maggi Seasoning, and bay leaf, bring back to a boil again, then stir and cover. Simmer for about 1-1/2 hours, adding more water if necessary. If all the potatoes have not broken down by the end of the cooking time, mash them with a potato masher or whisk. Season to taste with salt and pepper before serving.

Served with a crusty bread, this hearty low-fat soup makes a satisfying meal.

Serves 10 to 12

GINI'S HOME COOKING & BAKERY
7214 Blanco Road
San Antonio, Texas 78216
(210) 342-2768

☎ Sopa de Conchas

5 large cloves garlic, minced
3/4 pound tomatoes,
    quartered, plus 1 tomato,
    chopped
1 teaspoon dried basil or
    oregano
1-1/2 teaspoons ground cumin
1 bay leaf
1/4 onion (whole) plus 1/4
    onion (chopped)
1 (12-ounce) package pasta
    shells
1-1/2 cups vegetable oil
1 bunch green onions,
    chopped
1 stalk celery, chopped
1 medium green bell pepper,
    chopped
1/4 cup minced cilantro leaves
3 to 3-1/2 quarts chicken broth
1 teaspoon tomato paste
    (optional)
Salt and pepper to taste
5 ounces (1/2 of a 10-ounce
    bag) fresh spinach, rinsed
    and stems removed
1 cup shredded Monterey Jack
    cheese
1-1/2 to 2 cups pico de gallo

In a sauté pan, combine garlic, quartered tomatoes, basil or oregano, cumin, bay leaf, and 1/4 onion (whole). Mash tomatoes and simmer mixture in the juice. When tender, transfer mixture to a blender or food processor and whirl until blended. Set aside.

Deep-fry uncooked pasta shells in batches in hot vegetable oil until they turn light gold. Drain very well on paper towels and set aside.

In a stockpot, combine green onions, remaining 1/4 onion (chopped), celery, bell pepper, chopped tomato, cilantro, blended tomato mixture, and pasta. Stir in chicken broth, bring mixture to a boil, and simmer until pasta is tender (about 20 minutes). Add tomato paste for color, if desired, and salt and pepper to taste. To serve, place several leaves of spinach in individual soup bowls. Add soup, then top with 1 to 2 tablespoons grated cheese and 2 to 3 tablespoons pico de gallo.

Frying keeps the pasta from coming apart when added to the broth.

Serves 10

EL MIRADOR RESTAURANT
722 South St. Mary's Street
San Antonio, Texas 78205
(210) 225-9444

▨ Oaxacan Ajo Soup

6 cloves garlic, chopped finely
3 tablespoons olive oil
1 (28-ounce) can whole plum
  tomatoes
1 cup beef broth
1-1/2 teaspoons dried thyme
2 eggs, beaten
2 tablespoons tomato paste
4 tablespoons feta cheese and
1 julienned serrano chili

In a large saucepan, sauté garlic in olive oil until golden brown. Puree tomatoes in a blender or food processor and add to sautéed garlic, along with beef broth and thyme. Simmer for 30 to 45 minutes, stirring occasionally.

Bring mixture to a boil and slowly whisk in beaten eggs in a clockwise circular motion. Remove from heat and stir in tomato paste. Ladle into serving bowls and garnish with crumbled feta cheese and julienned serrano chili.

This soup is wonderful served hot or cold. It can be prepared up to 2 days before serving.

Serves 4

CAFE CAMILLE
517 East Woodlawn
San Antonio, Texas 78212
(210) 735-2307

☎ Menger Tortilla Soup

1/2 pound lean ground beef
3/4 cup chopped yellow onion
1 poblano chili, chopped
2 Anaheim chilies, chopped
1-1/4 cups diced tomatoes
1/2 cup tomato paste
3 quarts chicken stock
1/2–3/4 teaspoon ground
   cumin
4 sprigs cilantro, minced
1/2 teaspoon garlic powder
Salt and pepper to taste
Deep-fried tortilla strips,
   grated Monterey Jack
   cheese, and grated cheddar
   cheese

Brown ground beef in a large stockpot. Drain off fat, then add onion, chilies, and tomatoes. Sauté until just tender, then add tomato paste, continuing to sauté lightly (do not let paste brown or burn). Stir in chicken stock, cumin, cilantro, garlic powder, salt, and pepper. Bring to a boil, then simmer for 45 minutes. Skim off any fat, then adjust seasoning as necessary.

To serve, ladle soup into bowls and garnish each with 2 tablespoons tortilla strips, 1 teaspoon Monterey Jack cheese, and 1 teaspoon cheddar cheese.

This soup is so popular with customers that the Menger Hotel keeps it on the menu every day. It's the hotel's most requested recipe.

Serves 12

THE COLONIAL ROOM RESTAURANT
The Menger Hotel
204 Alamo Plaza
San Antonio, Texas 78205
(210) 223-4361

♠ Cactus Flower Tortilla Soup

3 cups beef stock
3 cups chicken stock
4 slices bacon, diced finely
1 large onion, diced
1 large tomato, diced
3/4 teaspoon ground cumin
3/4 teaspoon white pepper
1/2 cup loosely packed
   chopped cilantro
Match-size strips of crisply
   fried corn tortillas
Shredded Monterey Jack
   cheese and 2 tablespoons
   guacamole

Combine beef and chicken stocks in a pot and bring to a boil. Reduce heat and simmer gently. In a separate skillet, sauté bacon until browned and crisp. Drain off excess grease and add diced onions and tomatoes. Continue sautéing until onions are tender. Add cumin, white pepper, and chopped cilantro, mixing well. Stir mixture into beef-chicken stock and simmer for 10 minutes.

To serve, line the bottoms of 6 soup bowls with thin strips of crisp corn tortillas. Divide soup between bowls, then top each with a sprinkle of Monterey Jack cheese and a teaspoon of guacamole. Serve immediately.

The generous portion of cilantro gives this soup a fresh, exciting flavor.

Serves 6

CACTUS FLOWER CAFE
Marriott Riverwalk
711 East Riverwalk
San Antonio, Texas 78205
(210) 224-4555

☎ Caldo Xochitl

2 pounds boneless, skinless
   chicken breasts, cut into
   bite-sized pieces
3/4 gallon hot water
4 tablespoons (3 ounces)
   chicken base
3 cloves
2 large bay leaves
2-1/4 teaspoons ground cumin
1 tablespoon plus 1-1/2
   teaspoons dried oregano
3/4 teaspoon white pepper
1-1/2 teaspoons minced garlic
6 carrots, cut into 1/4-inch
   slices
1/2 large yellow onion,
   chopped coarsely
1 (15-ounce) can garbanzo
   beans, rinsed and drained
2 zucchini, cut into 1/4-inch
   slices
Leaves from 1/3 bunch
   cilantro, coarsely chopped
1 tablespoon dried basil

In a stockpot over high heat, combine hot water and chicken base. Add cloves, bay leaves, cumin, oregano, white pepper, and garlic, mixing well. When mixture comes to a boil, reduce heat to a simmer. Add carrots, onions, and garbanzo beans.

Continue to simmer mixture until carrots are tender, then immediately add chicken, zucchini, cilantro, and basil. As soon as chicken is cooked through (after about 5 to 8 minutes), remove soup from heat and serve.

This fragrant soup, loaded with chunks of chicken, zucchini, and carrots, is a San Antonio favorite. Serve with it hot rolls and butter or your choice of tortillas.

Serves 8 to 10

WATER STREET OYSTER BAR
999 East Basse, Suite 130
San Antonio, Texas 78209
(210) 829-4853

☎ Quick Tomato-Cheese Bisque with French Bread Croûtes

2 tablespoons butter or
   margarine
1 large carrot, sliced
1 medium onion, chopped
2 cloves garlic, flattened or
   chopped
1 (13-1/2-ounce) can chicken
   broth
1 (15-ounce) can tomato puree
   (or diced tomatoes in puree)
1/2 teaspoon pepper
2 fresh basil leaves, minced (or
   1 teaspoon dried basil), plus
   1/2 cup fresh basil leaves,
   slivered
1 cup heavy cream
1/2 cup crumbled blue cheese
   or goat cheese

In a 4-quart saucepan, melt butter and add carrot, onion, and garlic. Sauté until vegetables are slightly softened, then add chicken broth and tomato puree. Bring mixture to a boil, then reduce heat and simmer until onions and carrots are tender (about 10 minutes).

Transfer mixture to a blender or food processor, and whirl until smooth. Return mixture to pan, season with pepper and minced basil, and heat gently (do not boil). Just before serving, add cream and cheese, heating until combined. Adjust seasonings and top with slivered fresh basil and one or two **French Bread Croûtes.**

Even though made with canned tomatoes, this soup has a deceptive "garden fresh" taste.

Serves 6

French Bread Croûtes

12 thin slices French bread
Extra-virgin olive oil or butter

Brush bread slices with olive oil or butter. Toast under a broiler or in a toaster oven until browned.

These are good atop a variety of soups, particularly cream-based ones.

Makes 12

H-E-B MARKETPLACE
6501 Bandera Road
San Antonio, Texas 78238
(210) 647-2700

☖ Ernesto's Hot Sauce

1 pound (15–16) tomatillos, halved
1-1/2 teaspoons sugar
5 serrano chilies, stemmed and seeded
1 clove garlic, minced
2 tablespoons white vinegar
3/4 cup vegetable oil, heated
1/2 teaspoon salt, or to taste

In a medium saucepan, combine tomatillos, sugar, chilies, garlic, and vinegar. Bring to a boil, then reduce heat and simmer for 8 to 10 minutes (tomatillos turn dull green when tender).

Transfer cooked mixture to a blender or food processor and whirl until smooth and light (about 2 minutes). With machine still running, slowly pour oil through the tube. When all oil has been added, add salt. Serve hot or cold with tortilla chips, chilled shrimp, or seafood appetizers (keep unused portions refrigerated).

This table sauce is one of owner Ernesto Torres's most popular recipes. It can be stored in the refrigerator for up to 2 weeks.

Makes 3 cups

ERNESTO'S
2559 Jackson Keller
San Antonio, Texas 78230
(210) 344-1248

☎ Salsa de Tomatillo Miriam

1/2 small white onion, chopped finely
1 small clove garlic, chopped
1/3 cup water
2 cups chopped tomatillos
4 jalapeño chilies, or less to taste
6 large sprigs cilantro
1 large avocado, peeled and seeded
1/4 teaspoon salt, or to taste

Place onion, garlic, and water in a blender or food processor and whirl for a few seconds. Add half the tomatillos and the jalapeños. Process for a few more seconds, then add remaining tomatillos. Whirl again briefly, then add cilantro, avocado, and salt. Process just enough to incorporate all ingredients (do not overblend—there should be some texture and pieces of skin evident in the sauce).

The tomatillos keep the avocado from darkening, so this sauce keeps well for 2 to 3 days, but it's best when served fresh. Try it with tortilla chips, grilled meats, or other Mexican specialties.

Makes 3 cups

LA CALESA
2103 East Hildebrand
San Antonio, Texas 78209
(210) 822-4475

♠ Sizzling Expensive Mushrooms

1/4 pound oyster mushrooms
1/4 pound shiitake
   mushrooms, stems removed
   and sliced
1/4 pound Portobello
   mushrooms, stems removed
   and roughly chopped
1/4 pound chanterelle
   mushrooms
1/2 red onion, sliced
1-1/2 teaspoons minced garlic
2 tablespoons olive oil
1 teaspoon chopped fresh
   rosemary
1 teaspoon chopped fresh sage
1 teaspoon chopped fresh
   parsley
1/2 teaspoon chopped fresh
   thyme
1 tablespoon balsamic vinegar
A scant 1/2 cup dry white
   wine, or to taste
8 slices crusty bread, toasted
   on grill (optional)

Combine all ingredients except wine and bread in a nonmetallic bowl. Place a fajita sizzle pan or a cast-iron skillet on the grill and heat until pan becomes very hot. Empty mushroom mixture onto hot pan and close grill cover. Cook until mushrooms are tender (about 5 minutes). Remove from grill and splash with wine to sizzle. Serve on fajita sizzle pan with toasted bread slices.

The name may draw attention to these mushrooms, but it's the flavor that you'll remember.

Serves 3

RESTAURANT BIGA
206 East Locust Street
San Antonio, Texas 78212
(210) 225-0722

☎ Black Bean Tofu Nachos

1 cup finely shredded lettuce
1 tomato, diced finely
1/4 cup guacamole
1/4 cup sour cream (optional)
2 tablespoons chopped
    cilantro
2 tablespoons sliced jalapeños
    (fresh or pickled)
About 3 ounces (1/3 of a
    10-ounce container) firm
    tofu, cut into 24 equal
    pieces
2 red corn tortillas (substitute
    yellow if unavailable)
2 yellow corn tortillas
Vegetable oil
1 cup pureed black beans, well
    seasoned with salt and
    pepper
1 cup grated Colby Jack
    cheese

In the center of a large oval platter, attractively mound lettuce, tomato, and guacamole. Add sour cream, if desired, and garnish platter with 2 teaspoons each of cilantro and jalapeños.

Lightly toast tofu pieces on a griddle or in a sauté pan. Set aside. Deep-fry tortillas in hot oil until crunchy, then drain well on paper towels.

Preheat oven broiler. Spread black bean puree over tortillas and top with cheese. Place tortillas on a baking sheet and broil until cheese melts and bubbles. Cut each tortilla into 6 triangles, then place a piece of tofu on each triangle and arrange on the serving platter, alternating red and yellow triangles. Sprinkle with remaining cilantro and serve immediately.

This very colorful, festive dish would serve well as an appetizer at any dinner party, and it would surely be a hit at a vegetarian affair!

Serves 4 to 6

BOARDWALK BISTRO
4011 Broadway
San Antonio, Texas 78209
(210) 824-0100

☗ Emeterio's San Antonio Eggs with Tomatillo Sauce

1 tablespoon butter or
   margarine
6 large eggs, beaten and salted
   to taste
6 corn tortillas, cut into strips
   and fried in hot oil until
   crisp
3/4 cup shredded mozzarella
   cheese
3/4 cup shredded cheddar
   cheese

Prepare **Tomatillo Sauce** and set aside.

Preheat oven broiler. In a large, medium-hot skillet, melt butter, then add eggs and enough tortilla strips to cover the bottom. Stir gently (the trick is to scramble and cook the eggs without breaking up the chips). When eggs are mostly set, remove from heat and sprinkle with cheese. Transfer pan to oven and broil just long enough to melt cheese. Served topped generously with **Tomatillo Sauce.**

Serve these with your favorite breakfast potatoes, fresh fruit, and hot flour tortillas.

Serves 3 to 4

Tomatillo Sauce

1/2 pound tomatillos, husked
1 teaspoon minced garlic
1/2 small onion, chopped
4–6 serrano chilies
1/2 cup water
Salt to taste
1/4 bunch cilantro, stems
   removed, chopped

In a medium saucepan, combine tomatillos, garlic, onion, chilies, and water. Bring to a boil, then reduce heat and simmer for 5 minutes. Transfer mixture to a blender or food processor and puree. Reduce sauce over low heat if necessary—consistency should be that of a nice tomato sauce. Season with salt, stir in cilantro, and serve.

This sauce also can be used to top other Mexican specialties or as a dipping sauce for tortilla chips.

ZUNI GRILL
511 East Riverwalk
San Antonio, Texas 78205
(210) 227-0864

⌂ San Antonio Ceviche

1 pound medium shrimp,
  peeled and deveined
3/4 pound sea scallops
2/3 cup fresh lime or lemon
  juice, or less as needed
1 tomato, chopped
1 small yellow onion, minced
1 jalapeño chili, stemmed,
  seeded, and minced
2 tablespoons minced cilantro
2 tablespoons ketchup
5–6 drops Tabasco sauce
Tortilla chips

Blanch shrimp and scallops for 1-1/2 minutes in boiling water. Drain well, then chop into small pieces and place in a glass bowl. Add enough fresh lime or lemon juice to cover seafood, then add tomato, onion, jalapeño, cilantro, ketchup, and Tabasco sauce. Cover and refrigerate for at least 3 hours before serving with tortilla chips for dipping.

This recipe tastes best when made a day in ahead (it will keep in the refrigerator up to 3 days). If desired, serve the ceviche spooned over lettuce leaves and garnished with an avocado slice.

Serves 4 to 6

ERNESTO'S
2559 Jackson Keller
San Antonio, Texas 78230
(210) 344-1248

♚ Oysters Escabeche

1 pint oysters, shelled and in
    liquor
2 cloves garlic, minced
2 tablespoons olive oil
2 medium yellow onions,
    sliced very thinly and
    separated into rings
2 large carrots, julienned
1/4 cup capers
1/4 cup cider vinegar
1 tablespoon Italian seasoning
1/2 teaspoon pepper
Salt to taste
Lime wedges and crackers

Strain oysters and reserve liquor. In a large skillet, sauté garlic in olive oil. Add onions and cook but do not brown. When onions are translucent, add oysters and cook until just done (about 2 to 3 minutes). Add carrots and remove from the heat. Set aside.

In a separate pan, bring reserved oyster liquor just to a boil, then strain it. In a small bowl, combine strained liquor, oyster-carrot mixture, capers, vinegar, Italian seasoning, pepper, and salt. Cover and refrigerate mixture overnight or for at least 3 hours. Serve accompanied by lime wedges and crackers.

This dish can be prepared up to 2 days in advance as long as it is kept very cold but not frozen. Spring and fall are the best times to buy oysters, but they are fine in the summer as long as you buy from a reputable fish supplier.

Serves 3 to 4

POLO'S AT THE FAIRMOUNT
401 South Alamo Street
San Antonio, Texas 78205
(210) 224-8800

♨ Shrimp Ruffino's

16 extra-large shrimp, peeled
  and deveined
2 tablespoons chopped onion
3 tablespoons butter
2 cups sliced mushrooms
1 teaspoon minced garlic
2 tablespoons dry sherry
1 tablespoon dry white wine
3/4 cup heavy cream
Salt and pepper to taste
1/4 cup minced fresh basil
1 tablespoon minced fresh
  parsley

In a large skillet, sauté onion in 2 tablespoons butter for 1 minute, then add shrimp and sauté for 30 seconds. Stir in mushrooms, garlic, sherry, and white wine, and cook to evaporate off alcohol. Add cream and reduce liquid by half. Season with salt and pepper, then stir in remaining 1 tablespoon butter, basil, and parsley. Serve immediately.

This is Ruffino's signature dish; it's sure to become a favorite in your home as well. Serve as an appetizer in ramekins with plenty of garlic bread for dipping, or increase the serving size and use as an entree with rice pilaf.

Serves 4

RUFFINO'S RESTAURANT & BAR
9802 Colonnade
San Antonio, Texas 78230
(210) 641-6100

⌂ Chicken Formaggio Pizza

1 (4-ounce) boneless, skinless chicken breast half, baked or sautéed
2 tablespoons diced onion
1 teaspoon minced garlic
1 teaspoon olive oil
1 cup canned tomatoes, drained and diced
Pinch of salt
1/2 teaspoon dry basil
1 (12-inch) prebaked pizza crust
1/2 cup shredded fontina cheese
1/2 cup shredded mozzarella cheese
1/2 cup sliced mushrooms
1 tablespoon grated Parmesan cheese

Preheat oven to 450 degrees. Cut cooled chicken breast into 1/4-inch-wide strips. Sauté onion and garlic briefly in olive oil, then combine with tomatoes, salt, and basil. Spread tomato mixture over pizza crust, then lay chicken strips over tomatoes. Top with fontina and mozzarella cheeses, followed by sliced mushrooms, and then sprinkle with Parmesan cheese. Bake for about 8 minutes or until cheese is melted and crust is piping hot.

If desired, the chicken can be grilled rather than baked or sautéed.

Serves 4 to 6

THE OLIVE GARDEN ITALIAN RESTAURANT
849 East Commerce Street
San Antonio, Texas 78205
(210) 224-5956
7920 Interstate 35 North
San Antonio, Texas 78218
(210) 650-5883
6155 Northwest Loop 410
San Antonio, Texas 78201
(210) 520-7935
13730 San Pedro
San Antonio, Texas 78232
(210) 490-3411

☎ Quesadillas del Mundo

8 (8-inch) flour tortillas
1 (16-ounce) can black beans,
   rinsed and drained
2 ounces French Brie cheese,
   diced small
2 ounces mozzarella cheese
2 ounces sharp cheddar cheese
2 ounces Gouda cheese
Margarine
Guacamole
Pico de gallo

Place 4 tortillas on countertop. Place black beans in a food processor and lightly chop into a coarse paste. Remove and set aside.

Place cheeses into a blender or food processor and whirl until smooth. Using half the black bean paste, spread each of the 4 tortillas evenly. Spread each tortilla with a fourth of the cheese mixture. Spread remaining black bean paste evenly onto remaining 4 tortillas. Place these tortillas, bean-side down, onto cheese layer of first 4 tortillas.

In a hot skillet, melt a little margarine and grill quesadillas until they are heated through and cheeses are fully melted, making sure to turn and brown both sides. Cut into wedges and serve with guacamole and pico de gallo on the side.

After the quesadillas are assembled and before they are fried, they can be refrigerated, well covered, for several hours.

Serves 4 to 6

FIESTA TEXAS CATERING
17000 Interstate 10 West
San Antonio, Texas 78269
(210) 697-5164

♜ Chicken and Cheese Spring Rolls

5 boneless, skinless chicken
  breast halves, cut into small
  strips
1/4 cup (1/2 stick) butter
Salt and pepper to taste
3 eggs
2 tablespoons water
24 spring roll (not egg roll)
  wrappers (available at Asian
  markets)
12 ounces fontina cheese, cut
  into 12 slices
6 Roma tomatoes, peeled,
  seeded, and diced
24 sprigs cilantro
Vegetable oil

In a large skillet, sauté chicken in hot butter until cooked through. Season strips with salt and pepper and remove from pan with a slotted spoon. Cool and refrigerate.

In a small bowl, beat eggs and water together. Place 1 spring roll sheet in front of you with corner pointing down so that sheet looks like a diamond. Lightly brush sheet with egg mixture. Place 1 slice of cheese in bottom corner of brushed sheet and top with some cold chicken strips, diced tomatoes, and 2 sprigs of cilantro.

Pick up corner containing filling and carefully roll halfway. Next fold the 2 side corners inward and continue to roll. Brush another sheet with egg mixture and place finished roll on top of new one. Repeat roll-up procedure (each spring roll has two sheets, rolled individually). Repeat steps with remaining ingredients. Heat oil to 325 degrees and deep-fry rolls until golden brown.

These rolls can be made ahead and refrigerated, uncooked, for 2 days. The rice flour used in spring roll wrappers lends a delicious flavor and crispy texture, quite unlike that of an egg roll.

Serves 6

BISTRO TIME
5137 Fredericksburg Road
San Antonio, Texas 78229
(210) 344-6626

Main Courses

✿ Sonora Casserole

2 cups tomato sauce
1/4 teaspoon ground cumin
1-1/2 tablespoons chili powder
1/4 teaspoon cayenne pepper
1 tablespoon white vinegar
1/4 teaspoon granulated garlic
   or garlic powder
Salt to taste
6 corn tortillas
Hot vegetable oil
3 cups sliced fresh zucchini
1 cup fresh or frozen corn
   kernels
1 (4-ounce) can diced green
   chilies, drained
1-1/2 cups grated cheddar
   cheese
3/4 cup sour cream
2 green onions, sliced thinly

Preheat oven to 350 degrees. Combine tomato sauce, cumin, chili powder, cayenne pepper, vinegar, garlic, and salt in a pan. Heat and simmer gently.

Slice tortillas into 1/8-inch strips and fry in hot oil. Drain well.

Boil or steam zucchini until it is tender, then drain. In a large bowl, combine zucchini, tortilla strips, corn, green chilies, and 3/4 cup cheese. Spoon mixture into a well-greased 9-by-13-inch baking dish, then spread tomato sauce and remaining 3/4 cup cheese on top. Bake uncovered for about 30 minutes, or until mixture begins bubbling. Remove from oven and spread sour cream on top. Sprinkle with green onions and serve.

This delicious Southwestern-flavored casserole is a much-requested recipe at the 410 Diner. It can be served as a vegetarian entree or as a side dish.

Serves 8 as an entree, 12 to 16 as a side dish

410 DINER
8315 Broadway
San Antonio, Texas 78209
(210) 822-6246

✿ Black Bean Chili

2 cups dry black beans
1 bay leaf
1 tablespoon ground cumin
1 tablespoon dried oregano
1 tablespoon paprika
4 tablespoons vegetable oil
2 cups chopped onion
1 tablespoon minced garlic
1 teaspoon cayenne pepper
2 tablespoons chili powder
1 cup canned diced tomatoes
1-1/2 teaspoons salt
1 tablespoon red wine vinegar

Rinse beans in a colander, then place in a bowl. Add 7 to 8 cups of cold water, cover, and let stand for 24 hours.

Drain beans and transfer to a pot with enough water to cover by 2 inches. Add bay leaf and begin to simmer.

In a small skillet, heat cumin, oregano, and paprika until spices begin to color slightly (about 2 minutes). Set aside.

In a small pan, heat oil and sauté onion and garlic until soft (about 10 minutes). Add roasted spices, cayenne, and chili powder. Cook for 5 minutes, then add tomatoes and cook for 15 minutes more, stirring frequently. Add mixture to beans and stir in well. Make sure beans are covered by 1 inch of liquid; if not, add water. Simmer over low heat for 45 45 minutes, then add salt and continue cooking until beans are no longer tough (about 45 minutes more). Add vinegar and cook for 5 minutes, then adjust seasoning and serve.

This wonderful vegetarian chili has a delightful blend of flavors. It improves with age, so it can easily be made ahead (and frozen, if desired).

Serves 8

POUR LA FRANCE
7959 Broadway
San Antonio, Texas 78209
(210) 826-4333

⟐ Squash au Gratin

2-1/2 pounds zucchini, sliced
5 tablespoons butter
1/2 cup chopped onion
1/3 cup chopped green bell
    pepper
2 tablespoons tomato paste
1/2 teaspoon ground cumin
Dash of Tabasco sauce
Salt and pepper to taste
1/8 teaspoon sugar
1 cup grated cheddar cheese
1/2 cup fine bread crumbs

Preheat oven to 350 degrees. Boil zucchini in a small amount of salted water until tender-crisp. Drain off water, then using a wooden spoon, break zucchini into medium pieces. Set aside.

In 2 tablespoons butter, sauté onion and green peppers until onions are translucent. Add tomato paste and stir mixture into zucchini, followed by cumin, Tabasco, salt, pepper, and sugar. Transfer mixture to a shallow casserole, top with cheese, sprinkle with a layer of bread crumbs, and dot with the remaining 3 tablespoons butter. Bake for 20 to 25 minutes or until heated through.

This casserole can be completely assembled and refrigerated before baking (allow additional baking time).

Serves 4 as an entree, 6 as a side dish

GREY MOSS INN
19010 Scenic Loop Road
Helotes, Texas 78023
(210) 695-8301

⬙ Grey Moss Inn Potatoes on the Half Shell

4 large baking potatoes
Vegetable oil
1 egg
1 teaspoon salt
1/4 teaspoon pepper
1/2 cup warm milk
4 tablespoons melted butter
1/2 cup sour cream
1 tablespoon minced chives or
   green onion tops
Paprika

Preheat oven to 400 degrees. Wash and dry potatoes, then grease lightly with vegetable oil and bake for about 1 hour, or until tender. Set aside to cool slightly.

Halve potatoes lengthwise and carefully scoop flesh into a mixing bowl. Leave some potato flesh (approximately 1/4 inch) on the skin to make a sturdy "boat." Reserve hollowed skins for filling.

Heat oven to 350 degrees. Whip egg, salt, pepper, milk, butter, and sour cream with potato flesh until mixture is smooth. Stir in chives. Fill potato skins with mixture, sprinkle with paprika, and arrange on a baking sheet. Bake for 20 to 25 minutes, or until heated through.

For a tasty variation, add 1/2 cup grated cheddar cheese or 1/2 cup crisply fried bacon morsels after the potato mixture has been whipped. The potatoes also can be topped with grated cheese before baking.

Serves 8

GREY MOSS INN
19010 Scenic Loop Road
Helotes, Texas 78023
(210) 695-8301

Jalapeño Potatoes

8 unbaked Grey Moss Inn
Potatoes on the Half Shell
(see recipe on page 50)
1 medium white onion, finely
chopped
1-1/2 tablespoons melted
unsalted butter, plus
additional to brush tops of
potatoes
4–5 whole pickled jalapeño
chilies
8 slices bacon, crisply baked or
fried and crumbled
2/3 cup grated cheddar cheese
2/3 cup grated mozzarella
cheese
Paprika

Match up unbaked **Grey Moss Inn Pota-toes on the Half Shell** by pairs, so that 2 potato halves will form a whole potato. Refrigerate for 2 to 3 hours to set filling.

Preheat oven to 350 degrees. Sauté onion in butter until tender. Set aside. Chop jalapeños with seeds in a food processor or by hand. Using 1 potato half from each pair, distribute onions, jalapeños, bacon, and cheeses equally over the 4 potato halves. Place top half of potatoes onto bottom halves and mold potatoes together at the seams. Place on a greased baking sheet, brush with melted butter, and sprinkle with paprika. Bake for 30 to 45 minutes, or until heated through.

This makes a delicious, filling entree or a side dish.

Serves 4

GREY MOSS INN
19010 Scenic Loop Road
Helotes, Texas 78023
(210) 695-8301

⚘ Texas Quiche

2/3 cup cubed cooked chicken
1/3 cup sliced mushrooms
2 small carrots, sliced thinly
1 tablespoon butter,
    margarine, or vegetable oil
8 eggs
1/2 teaspoon white pepper
1/2 teaspoon salt
1 teaspoon ground cumin
2 teaspoons sliced pickled
    jalapeño chilies with liquid
2 cups evaporated milk
2 cups grated Monterey Jack
    cheese
1/2 cup canned whole green
    chilies, drained and sliced
    into strips
Sour cream and black olives

Prepare **Basic Quiche Crust** and set aside.

Preheat oven to 350 degrees. Sauté mushrooms and carrots in butter. Remove from heat and set aside. Beat eggs in a blender with white pepper, salt, cumin, and jalapeños. Add milk to egg mixture and set aside.

Place half of cheese on the bottom of prepared crust. Layer with mushrooms and carrots, green chilies, and chicken. Sprinkle with remaining cheese, then pour egg mixture over layered ingredients. Bake quiche for 85 to 95 minutes, or until a knife inserted in the center comes out clean. Allow quiche to cool for 15 minutes for easier slicing, then garnish each slice with a dollop of sour cream and a black olive.

Small wonder this is called "Texas" quiche—it's oversized, just like the state. Chicken, green chilies, and a touch of cumin flavor make this a favorite with tea room customers.

Serves 10

Basic Quiche Crust

1-1/2 cups unsifted
   unbleached all-purpose
   flour
1/2 teaspoon salt
2 tablespoons shortening
6 tablespoons chilled butter
5 tablespoons ice water

Preheat oven to 400 degrees. Mix flour and salt in a medium bowl, then cut in shortening and butter with a pastry blender until crumbly. Add water, a little at a time, mixing with a fork until well blended. Place dough into a resealable plastic bag and gently press into a flat disk. Seal bag and refrigerate for 30 to 60 minutes.

On a floured board, carefully roll dough out to fit a large quiche pan (10-by-2-inches-deep). Carefully lift dough into pan, trimming and rolling the edge under to form a ridge. Flute edges. Place a sheet of aluminum foil over dough and fill pan to the top with pie weights or dry pinto beans. Bake crust for 15 minutes. Remove beans and foil, prick crust bottom several times with a fork, and bake for 10 minutes more.

Makes 1 crust

THE PEACH TREE GIFT GALLERY AND TEA ROOM
210 South Adams Street
Fredericksburg, Texas 78624
(210) 997-9527

✿ Mexican-Style Fettuccine

16 ounces uncooked fettuccine
2 tablespoons olive oil
1/2 cup (1 stick) plus
   2 tablespoons butter
1 cup plus 2 tablespoons
   freshly grated Parmesan
   cheese
3 large poblano chilies
2 cups sour cream
1/4 cup half-and-half
2 tablespoons Knorr Swiss
   chicken granules

Cook fettuccine in salted water to which olive oil has been added until al dente. Drain pasta and run cold water over it to remove starch. Transfer pasta to a large shallow bowl and set aside.

In a skillet, melt (but do not brown) 1/2 cup butter. Remove from heat and set aside. Scatter 1 cup Parmesan cheese over pasta and toss with hands to get cheese well embedded. Pour melted butter over pasta and set aside.

Put poblano chilies on a grill and heat until well blistered. Place in a sealed plastic bag for 5 minutes, then peel under cold running water and remove seeds. Transfer chilies onto paper towels to absorb water. When chilies are well drained, place in a blender or food processor and top with sour cream and half-and-half. Add chicken granules and whirl until blended. (If mixture is too thick, add a little more cream.)

Add chili mixture to fettuccine along with remaining 2 tablespoons Parmesan cheese and combine well. Top with 2 tablespoons butter, cut into little pats. Heat in a 350-degree oven (about 10 minutes) or a microwave until hot and bubbly.

This can be served as a vegetarian entree or it makes a delicious side dish with grilled steak or poultry. Teka Molino uses Knorr Caldo de Pollo, the Mexican version of the Swiss chicken granules.

Serves 6

TEKA MOLINO
7231 San Pedro
San Antonio, Texas 78216
(210) 344-7281
2403 North St. Mary's Street
San Antonio, Texas 78212
(210) 735-5471

ᛥ Creamed Pasta with Fresh Basil

8 ounces thin, flat pasta (such as linguine), cooked al dente
1 large clove garlic
15 fresh basil leaves
1 cup half-and-half or light cream
2 tablespoons unsalted butter
Salt and freshly ground pepper to taste
1-1/3 cups grated Gruyère cheese

Mince together garlic and basil with scissors or chop on a board. Using the still-hot saucepan the pasta cooked in, pour in half-and-half, butter, basil-garlic mixture, salt, pepper, and pasta. Reheat and serve immediately, accompanied by a bowl of grated Gruyère.

Fresh basil may be difficult to obtain in the winter. If so, substitute another fresh herb or use pesto.

Serves 2 to 4

LA MADELEINE FRENCH BAKERY & CAFE
4820 Broadway
San Antonio, Texas 78209
(210) 829-7279

Shrimp Fettuccine

16 ounces fresh or 12 ounces
  dry fettuccine, cooked al
  dente
1 pound large shrimp, peeled
  and deveined
2 teaspoons minced garlic
3 tablespoons olive oil
1 cup dry white wine
1-1/3 cups heavy cream
1-1/2 teaspoons dried thyme
Salt and pepper to taste

In a medium saucepan over high heat, quickly sauté shrimp and garlic in olive oil. Add wine and cream, then reduce liquid by half over medium heat. Add thyme, salt, and pepper, followed by cooked fettuccine. Mix well, then transfer to a serving dish.

A grating of fresh Parmesan cheese makes this tasty dish even more special.

Serves 4

CRUMPETS
5800 Broadway, Suite 302
San Antonio, Texas 78209
(210) 821-5600

Shrimp and Penne Pasta with Balsamic Cream

1 pound medium shrimp, peeled and deveined (tails left on)
16 ounces penne or rigatoni pasta, cooked al dente
6 ancho chilies
1/2 cup olive oil
3 cloves garlic, minced
1/4 cup plus 2 tablespoons balsamic vinegar
1/2 cup dry white wine
2 cups heavy cream
6 Roma tomatoes, quartered lengthwise
25 leaves fresh basil, chopped coarsely, plus 12 whole leaves to garnish
Salt and freshly ground pepper to taste
Freshly grated Parmesan cheese

Remove seeds and stems from ancho chilies and place chilies in boiling water for 10 minutes. Drain and transfer chilies to a blender or food processor and puree until they develop a paste-like consistency. Set aside.

In a large skillet, sauté shrimp in 1/4 cup olive oil. When shrimp turn opaque, remove them from the pan. Add remaining olive oil and garlic to pan, and sauté but do not brown. Add ancho puree, vinegar, and wine, and heat to reduce by half. Stir in heavy cream and tomatoes, and continue heating to reduce mixture to sauce consistency (about 5 minutes). Reduce heat to warm, then add pasta, shrimp, and chopped basil to sauce and toss. Season with salt and pepper. Serve garnished with Parmesan cheese and whole basil leaves.

Balsamic vinegar adds an exquisite flavor to this dish. The sauce reheats nicely, but cook the pasta at serving time.

Serves 6

CAFE CAMILLE
517 East Woodlawn
San Antonio, Texas 78212
(210) 735-2307

Gulf Shrimp Pasta with Bacon, Sweet Corn, and Red Peppers

1/2 pound medium shrimp, peeled and deveined

4 slices bacon, cut into 1/4-inch pieces

12 ounces fresh rotini or raddiatore (or 8 ounces dry short and curly pasta), cooked al dente

1/2 large onion, diced large

3 ears corn, roasted on grill and kernels cut off (or a 10-ounce package frozen corn, thawed)

2 roasted red peppers (or 1 red bell pepper), cut into 1/3-inch dice

4 slices jalapeño chili, chopped

1 tablespoon all-purpose flour

1 (14-1/2-ounce) can chicken broth

1 tablespoon chopped cilantro, plus additional leaves to garnish

Salt and pepper to taste

Tabasco sauce to taste

1/4 cup freshly grated Parmesan cheese

In a large skillet, fry bacon until crisp, then set aside to drain on a paper towel. Leave 1 tablespoon bacon drippings in pan and discard remainder.

Over medium heat, sauté shrimp, onion, corn, half the red peppers, and jalapeño in bacon drippings for 2 to 3 minutes. Stir in flour and cook for 2 to 3 minutes more, then add chicken broth, chopped cilantro, and half the bacon. Stir well, bring mixture to a boil, and simmer slowly for 5 to 10 minutes. Add drained pasta to sauce, then stir in remaining half of red peppers. Toss together just until combined, then season to taste (preferably highly seasoned) with salt, pepper, and Tabasco sauce. Place in large pasta bowls and top with grated cheese, then garnish with more black pepper and some cilantro leaves.

This unique pasta dish was created by Nancy Lazara, vice president of product development, who holds a Grande Diplôme from the prestigious Cordon Bleu cooking school. Although the dish is best prepared with roasted corn, frozen corn substitutes nicely.

Serves 3 to 4

H-E-B MARKETPLACE
6501 Bandera Road
San Antonio, Texas 78238
(210) 647-2700

☙ Crab Linguine

12 ounces linguine or
    fettuccine, cooked al dente
3/4–1 pound jumbo Texas
    lump crabmeat
1 tablespoon olive oil
2 shallots, sliced very thin
1 clove garlic, minced
1 tomato, diced
6 large basil leaves, julienned
Juice of 1/2 lime
1-1/2 to 2 cups clam juice
Salt and pepper to taste
1-1/2 tablespoons butter

Heat a large sauté pan very hot, then add oil and heat through. Stir in crab, shallots, garlic, tomatoes, and basil. Cook until all ingredients are just heated through, then deglaze pan with lime juice. Add clam juice immediately (the amount depends on how much liquid you like with your pasta). Stir in salt and pepper, then butter. Add cooked linguine and toss. Serve immediately in pasta bowls.

Serve this with a good warm French bread. The best Texas crabmeat is available May through September.

Serves 4

POLO'S AT THE FAIRMOUNT
401 South Alamo Street
San Antonio, Texas 78205
(210) 224-8800

⬛ Courtyard Grilled Chicken and Spinach Fettuccine Gorgonzola

4 boneless, skinless chicken breast halves, lightly marinated in olive oil, minced garlic, fresh thyme, and pepper
16 ounces fresh spinach fettuccine, cooked al dente
2 shallots, minced
2 tablespoons butter
2 cloves garlic, minced
2 slices bacon, cooked and diced
1/4 cup dry white wine
1/2 cup chicken stock
2 cups heavy cream
8 ounces Gorgonzola cheese, crumbled
1/2 cup freshly grated Parmesan cheese
3 tablespoons chopped fresh thyme
Salt and freshly ground pepper to taste
Diced tomatoes and thyme sprigs

Grill or smoke chicken just until done and cut into thin strips. Set aside.

Heat a large sauté pan and sauté shallots in butter for 2 minutes. Add garlic and sauté for 1 minute, then add bacon. Stir in wine to deglaze pan and reduce liquid by half. Add chicken stock, reduce by half again, and then add cream. Reduce cream by half and very slowly whisk in Gorgonzola. Add Parmesan very slowly, followed by chopped thyme and chicken strips. Season with salt and pepper.

Toss pasta with sauce and serve immediately in a pasta bowl or on a large plate. Garnish with diced tomatoes and fresh thyme sprigs.

If available, applewood-smoked bacon adds a special flavor to this dish.

Serves 4

THE COURTYARD AT LA LOU
2632 Broadway
San Antonio, Texas 78212
(210) 225-7987

✿ Villa Italian Lasagna

12 lasagna noodles, cooked al
  dente
1-1/2 pounds lean ground beef
1 large onion, chopped
1 clove garlic, minced
1 (16-ounce) can tomatoes
  with liquid
1 (15-ounce) can tomato sauce
1/4 cup minced fresh parsley
  (or 2 tablespoons dried
  flakes)
2 tablespoons sugar
1 teaspoon salt
1 teaspoon dried basil
1 (15-ounce) container ricotta
  cheese
1/4 cup fresh bread crumbs
2-1/2 cups grated mozzarella
  cheese

Cook ground beef, onion, and garlic in a large skillet or Dutch oven until meat is browned and onion is tender. Drain well. Place tomatoes with liquid in a blender or food processor and chop (do not puree). Transfer along with tomato sauce, parsley, sugar, salt, and basil to skillet containing meat and onion. Bring to a boil, then reduce heat and simmer for 1 hour or until mixture develops the consistency of spaghetti sauce. Remove from heat and set aside.

Preheat oven to 350 degrees. Place 3 lasagna noodles on the bottom of 9-by-13-inch baking dish. Top with ricotta cheese, then 3 more noodles. Reserve 1-1/2 cups meat sauce and set aside. Add bread crumbs to remaining sauce and spread mixture over noodles. Top with 3 more noodles, then sprinkle mozzarella cheese evenly over all. Top with 3 more noodles, followed by reserved meat sauce. Bake uncovered for 40 to 50 minutes. Let lasagna stand for 10 to 15 minutes after removing from oven for easier cutting.

If desired, the top of the lasagna may be sprinkled with freshly grated Parmesan cheese before serving. This dish freezes well, plus the meat sauce is also delicious over spaghetti.

Serves 12

VILLA ITALIAN SPECIALTIES
910 North Star Mall
San Antonio, Texas 78216
(210) 342-3428

✸ Shrimp Scampi

16 colossal shrimp (about 1 to
    1-1/4 pounds), peeled and
    deveined (tails left on)
All-purpose flour
5 tablespoons clarified butter
2-1/4 teaspoons minced garlic
Salt and pepper to taste
Scant 1/2 teaspoon paprika
5 teaspoons chopped fresh
    parsley
1/4 teaspoon dried oregano
1-1/2 cups dry white wine
4-1/2 teaspoons fresh lemon
    juice
6 tablespoons cold unsalted
    butter

Dust shrimp on both sides with flour. Heat clarified butter in a sauté pan until hot, then add shrimp, making sure they do not touch each other while sautéing. When crisp on one side, turn and brown shrimp on the other side. Drain off butter from skillet and add garlic, salt, pepper, paprika, parsley, and oregano. Sauté garlic only a few seconds, then add wine and lemon juice and simmer for about 4 minutes.

Remove shrimp and let liquid cook and reduce by half. When reduced, stir in cold butter to thicken sauce (do not let mixture boil or it will separate). Pour sauce over sautéed shrimp and serve.

Serve this with steamed vegetables and crusty bread so that you can soak up every bit of the delicious sauce. Although colossal shrimp work best for this dish, they are difficult to find, so substitute jumbo size if need be.

Serves 2 to 4

BOCACCIO RISTORANTE ITALIANO
205 North Presa Street
San Antonio, Texas 78205
(210) 225-1500

❀ Sauté Shrimp Haiti

24 extra-large shrimp, peeled
   and deveined
1 tablespoon extra-virgin olive
   oil
1 tablespoon unsalted butter
1/2 red bell pepper, chopped
   finely
1/2 green bell pepper,
   chopped finely
1 small onion, chopped finely
1 cup shiitake mushrooms,
   sliced thinly
1 tomato, peeled and diced
   finely
1-1/2 teaspoons curry powder
2 tablespoons cognac or
   brandy
1/2 cup heavy cream
Salt and pepper to taste
1 tablespoon chopped parsley

Heat olive oil and butter in a sauté pan until very hot. Add shrimp and sauté quickly on both sides. Add bell peppers, onion, and mushrooms, and sauté for 3 to 4 minutes. Stir in tomato and curry powder and cook for 2 minutes more. Add brandy or cognac and cook 2 minutes more, then add cream, salt, and pepper. Continue heating to reduce sauce by half. Transfer mixture to a hot plate, sprinkle with parsley, and serve.

Prepare white rice or your favorite pasta to serve alongside this flavorful shrimp.

Serves 6

FIG TREE RESTAURANT
515 Paseo De La Villita
San Antonio, Texas 78205
(210) 224-1976

⚜ Shrimp Margarita

12 jumbo shrimp, peeled and deveined (tails left on)
1/2 cup tequila
2 cups heavy cream
1 cup fish stock
3 large cloves garlic, minced
1/4 cup minced green bell pepper
1/4 cup minced red bell pepper
1 tablespoon grated lime zest
1 tablespoon grated lemon zest
1 tablespoon grated orange zest
1/2 cup minced cilantro
1 cup (2 sticks) butter, room temperature, cubed, plus 2 tablespoons cold butter
Salt and pepper to taste

Place tequila, cream, fish stock, and garlic in a saucepan. Heat and reduce liquid by three-fourths. Add peppers, zests, and cilantro, stir, and remove from heat. Whisk in softened butter, 1 piece at a time, until all is incorporated. Season with salt and pepper.

Place 2 tablespoons cold butter in a sauté pan. Sauté shrimp 6 at a time for 1 minute on each side or until done (do not let shrimp touch each other while cooking). Arrange shrimp on 2 dinner plates (tails pointing in), cover each with 1/4 cup sauce, and serve.

This is lovely garnished with kale and fresh fruit.

Serves 2

TOWER OF THE AMERICAS
222 Hemisfair Plaza
San Antonio, Texas 78210
(210) 223-3101

✺ Shrimp Venustiano

1 pound extra-large shrimp,
   peeled and deveined (tails
   left on)
2 eggs
2 cups milk
Salt and pepper to taste
All-purpose flour
Vegetable oil
8 ounces fettuccine, cooked al
   dente
Venustiano Sauce (see recipe
   on page 69)

In a shallow bowl, combine eggs, milk, salt, and pepper. Dip shrimp in mixture, then flour lightly. Heat vegetable oil in a sauté pan, then add shrimp 6 at a time (give shrimp plenty of room in the pan for cooking so that they sauté, not steam). Brown on one side, then turn and brown on the other. Shrimp can be finished off in a 350-degree oven or in the sauté pan. To serve, arrange shrimp atop a bed of fettuccine and top with **Venustiano Sauce.**

Restaurant patrons clamor for this recipe; it is one of Carranza's most popular offerings. As an appetizer, serve the shrimp on a bed of lemon slices and top with Venustiano Sauce.

Serves 3

CARRANZA GROCERY & MARKET
701 Austin Street
San Antonio, Texas 78215
(210) 223-0903

❧ Texas Crab Cakes with Herbed Tartar Sauce

1 pound jumbo lump crabmeat
1-1/2 cups fresh bread crumbs
1/2 teaspoon celery salt
3 egg whites
1/4 cup (1/2 stick) butter

The day before serving, prepare **Herb Mayonnaise** and **Herbed Tartar Sauce**.

Handle crabmeat very gently while removing as many shells as possible. Place meat in a large bowl, add bread crumbs and celery salt, and toss lightly. Add 3 tablespoons **Herb Mayonnaise** and egg whites, mixing gently (if mixture is dry, add more **Herb Mayonnaise** or egg whites). Form mixture into 6 patties. Heat butter in a skillet and sauté crab cakes on both sides until golden brown. Serve with **Herbed Tartar Sauce**.

The fine lump crabmeat makes these a special treat.

Serves 3

Herb Mayonnaise

1 (16-ounce) jar mayonnaise
5 sprigs fresh parsley, chopped
3 sprigs fresh basil, chopped
3 sprigs fresh dill, chopped
1/4 cup red wine vinegar

Whisk together all ingredients in a glass bowl. Refrigerate any unused portions (keeps up to 4 days).

Makes about 2 cups

Herbed Tartar Sauce

1-3/4 cups Herb Mayonnaise
1/3 cup capers
2 hard-cooked eggs, chopped
1 small onion, diced
1/4 cup diced dill pickle
1 tablespoon chopped fresh
   tarragon

Place all ingredients in a medium glass bowl and mix well. Refrigerate overnight before using (refrigerated sauce will keep for 4 days).

This can be served with any fried fish or as a sandwich spread.

Makes about 2 cups

BISTRO TIME
5137 Fredericksburg Road
San Antonio, Texas 78229
(210) 344-6626

❀ Carranza's Sea Cakes with Two Sauces

1 (10-ounce) fillet red snapper
1/3 pound medium or large
  shrimp (unpeeled)
1 (8-ounce) fillet whitefish
1/2 pound crabmeat, well
  picked
2 tablespoons butter
1 small onion, diced
1/2 red bell pepper, diced
1/2 yellow bell pepper, diced
1/2 green bell pepper, diced
2 tablespoons olive oil
Salt and pepper to taste
1-3/4 cups fine crumbs from
  day-old corn bread
1-3/4 cups dried white or
  wheat bread crumbs
2/3 cup buttermilk
2/3 cup heavy cream
2 eggs
2 tablespoons plus 2 teaspoons
  all-purpose flour
3 tablespoons sour cream
1/4 cup vegetable oil

Preheat oven to 350 degrees. Place snapper, shrimp, and whitefish in a baking pan and dot lightly with butter. Bake until tender (about 10 to 15 minutes). Cool in refrigerator. Peel shrimp and chop coarsely, cut fish into 1/2-inch pieces, and set all aside.

Sauté onion and bell peppers in olive oil until tender, then season with salt and pepper and cool in refrigerator.

Combine corn bread crumbs and bread crumbs, and set aside. In a medium bowl, mix together buttermilk, cream, eggs, flour, sour cream, salt, and pepper. Measure out 1-1/2 cups of cream mixture into another bowl and stir in onion-bell pepper mixture, crabmeat, shrimp, and fish. Mix with fingers, breaking up seafood while mixing (do not mix too well; fish and seafood pieces should be large enough to recognize). Mix in 2 to 4 handfuls of combined bread crumbs until mixture holds together (but is not dry). If needed, add additional cream mixture or bread crumbs. Form mixture into balls, then patties. Dip into bread crumb mixture, then refrigerate for 1 hour.

Fry patties in hot vegetable oil, turning once to brown both sides. Drain and serve on plates covered with **Venustiano Sauce**, then top with **Green Sauce**.

These sea cakes are Carranza's signature dish. Although the preparation is lengthy, much of it can be done ahead of time, and the flavor is well worth the effort.

Serves 6

Venustiano Sauce

1-1/2 cups (3 sticks) cold
 butter, cut into pieces
Juice of 1 medium lemon
3/4 teaspoon minced garlic
1-1/2 tablespoons minced
 fresh parsley

Combine butter, lemon juice, and garlic in a heavy saucepan. Over medium low heat, whisk constantly until butter is just melted and thickened. Stir in parsley, then remove from heat.

This sauce is delightful served with any type of broiled, grilled, or fried seafood.

Makes about 1-1/2 cups

Green Sauce

1 pound tomatillos, husked
1/2 bunch cilantro (2-1/2
 ounces), stems trimmed
1/3 bunch parsley (2-1/2
 ounces), stems trimmed
1/2 white onion
6 cloves garlic
3/4 teaspoon salt
1/4 teaspoon pepper
5 tablespoons olive oil

In a food processor fitted with a metal blade, grind tomatillos, cilantro, parsley, onion, and garlic. Transfer to a saucepan and add salt, pepper, and olive oil. Bring to a boil, then reduce heat and simmer for 20 minutes.

This also makes a wonderful dipping sauce for corn chips or a general-purpose salsa served with any kind of Mexican entree.

Makes about 2-1/2 cups

CARRANZA GROCERY & MARKET
701 Austin Street
San Antonio, Texas 78215
(210) 223-0903

⚜ Broiled Bacon-Wrapped Sea Scallops with Apricot Chutney

12 large sea scallops (about 1 pound)
12 slices bacon
2 tablespoons melted butter
8 spinach leaves
2 lemons, halved

Preheat oven to 350 degrees. Place bacon strips on a wire rack in a pan and bake until half done (about 13 minutes). Remove from oven and wrap 1 bacon slice around each scallop. Slide 3 bacon-wrapped scallops onto each of four 8-inch bamboo skewers, leaving a 1-inch gap between scallops.

Preheat oven broiler. Transfer skewered scallops to a greased pie pan and brush lightly with melted butter. Broil for 8 minutes, turning once after 4 minutes (watch carefully to avoid overcooking or burning scallops).

To serve, place 2 spinach leaves in the centers of 4 plates. Place 2 tablespoons of **Apricot Chutney** on 1 spinach leaf on each plate. Place 1 lemon half on each plate. Remove skewers and arrange 3 scallops on top of remaining spinach leaf on each plate. Serve immediately.

These are also good served with Herbed Tartar Sauce (see page 67).

Serves 4

Apricot Chutney

1 cup Smuckers apricot
 marmalade
1/2 cup prepared horseradish,
 strained
1-2 teaspoons freshly cracked
 pepper

In a stainless steel bowl, smooth marmalade with a wire whisk, then add horseradish and pepper. Blend thoroughly and refrigerate tightly covered for up to 3 weeks.

Makes 1-1/4 cups

MORTON'S OF CHICAGO, THE STEAKHOUSE
849 East Commerce Street
San Antonio, Texas 78205
(210) 228-0700

Marinated Scallops en Brochette

1 pound sea scallops
1/4 cup olive oil
2 tablespoons fresh lemon
    juice
2 tablespoons chopped parsley
1/2 teaspoon fennel seed
1 medium clove garlic, minced
2 tablespoons grated orange
    zest
1 medium zucchini
1 medium red onion

In a medium nonmetallic shallow bowl, whisk together olive oil, lemon juice, parsley, fennel seeds, garlic, and orange zest. Add scallops and toss well, then cover and refrigerate for at least 4 hours or overnight.

Preheat oven broiler. Slice zucchini into 1/4-inch pieces, then quarter onion and cut into small wedges. Thread scallops onto 4 lightly greased long metal skewers, alternating with zucchini and onion. Lay skewers on the rack of a broiler pan and broil 4 to 5 inches from heat, turning once or twice, until scallops are just opaque and done (about 5 to 10 minutes, depending on size of scallops). Transfer to heated dinner plates and serve.

A mixture of long grain and wild rice, rice pilaf, or saffron rice makes a nice accompaniment to these scallops.

Serves 4

STETSON RESTAURANT
Hilton Palacio del Rio Hotel
200 South Alamo Street
San Antonio, Texas 78205
(210) 222-1400

⟁ Ruth's Chris Trout Pecan

2 (10-ounce) trout fillets
Salt and pepper to taste
1 cup bread crumbs
1/3 cup vegetable oil
1/2 cup pecans, toasted and
  chopped
Chopped parsley and lemon
  wedges

Season trout with salt and pepper and dredge in bread crumbs. Heat oil in an iron skillet over medium heat until hot, then add fish. Fry for about 3 minutes until golden, then turn and brown on the other side (about 2 to 3 minutes more). Drain well.

Place fish on a platter, sprinkle with pecans, and top with 2 to 4 tablespoons of **Trout Pecan Sauce**. Garnish with parsley and lemon wedges.

The pecans can be roasted up to 5 days in advance and stored in an airtight container.

Serves 2

Trout Pecan Sauce

1/2 cup (1 stick) butter, cut
  into pieces
2 tablespoons Worcestershire
  sauce
Juice of 2 lemons

Combine all ingredients in a small saucepan and heat over medium heat, whisking constantly. When sauce starts to simmer, remove from heat and serve.

This sauce can also be served with other types of sautéed or grilled fish.

Makes 1/2 cup

RUTH'S CHRIS STEAK HOUSE
7720 Jones-Maltsberger, Suite 118
San Antonio, Texas 78216
(210) 821-5051

⟐ Thai Vegetable Salad with Grilled Salmon and Sesame-Ginger Dressing

6 (4-ounce) salmon fillets

1 cup julienned shiitake mushrooms

6 cups shredded spinach

1 cup chopped roasted cashews

1/2 cup chopped shallots

1/2 cup julienned red bell peppers

1/2 cup julienned yellow bell peppers

1 cup julienned carrots

1 cup julienned cucumbers

1 cup julienned asparagus, lightly blanched

1/4 package wonton skins, cut into 1/4-inch strips, fried in hot oil until crispy, and drained

1-1/2 ounces (1/6 of a 10-ounce package) rice sticks (rice-flour noodles), fried in hot oil until crisp and puffy, and drained

In a glass baking dish or a large resealable plastic bag, marinate salmon in 2/3 cup **Sesame-Ginger Dressing** for 1 hour. Remove fish from marinade and cook on a grill or in a heavy skillet over high heat until barely soft to the touch (about 4 minutes on each side). Set aside and keep warm.

In a small skillet, sauté mushrooms over medium heat in 2 tablespoons **Sesame-Ginger Dressing** until barely warmed (about 3 minutes). In a large bowl, combine mushrooms with spinach, cashews, shallots, bell peppers, carrots, cucumber, and asparagus, and toss with remaining **Sesame-Ginger Dressing**. When ingredients are well coated, gently toss in wontons and rice sticks (these will remain crisp only for a short time). Arrange salads on 6 plates and top with grilled salmon.

This salad is a visual and taste delight, thanks to generous additions of fresh, colorful vegetables. The rice sticks and wonton skins can be fried earlier in the day, drained thoroughly, and stored in a paper bag until serving time.

Serves 6

Sesame-Ginger Dressing

1/2 cup unseasoned rice wine
 vinegar
1/2 cup sugar
1/4 cup soy sauce
1 tablespoon minced fresh
 ginger
1 tablespoon chopped shallots
2 tablespoons minced garlic
2 tablespoons chopped green
 onions
1 tablespoon toasted sesame
 seeds
1 tablespoon sambal olek
 (available at Asian markets)
 or similar hot chili sauce
Juice of 1 lime
1/4 cup peanut oil
2 tablespoons sesame oil
Salt and white pepper to taste

Combine all ingredients except oils, salt, and pepper, and whisk together well. Slowly pour in oils while continuing to whisk. Season with salt and pepper.

Don't hesitate to use this flavorful dressing with other greens, or with cucumbers for an Asian-flavored side dish.

Makes about 2-1/4 cups

RESTAURANT BIGA
206 East Locust Street
San Antonio, Texas 78212
(210) 225-0722

Red Snapper Veracruz

4 (8-ounce) red snapper fillets
1/2 cup all-purpose flour
    seasoned with 1/2 teaspoon
    salt and 1/4 teaspoon pepper
1/4 cup olive oil
2 tablespoons chopped garlic
1/2 cup diced onion
1/2 cup diced green bell
    pepper
1/2 cup diced tomato
2 tablespoons capers
1/2 cup sliced green olives
1 teaspoon dried oregano
    leaves
2/3 cup picante sauce
Salt and pepper to taste
1/4 cup sliced jalapeño chilies
    (optional)
Parsley sprigs

Dust snapper fillets with flour mixture. Heat 2 tablespoons olive oil in a skillet and sauté snapper until lightly browned on both sides. Set skillet aside.

Pour remaining olive oil into a separate skillet and sauté garlic, onion, bell pepper, tomato, capers, olives, and oregano until vegetables are tender. Add remaining ingredients (except parsley) to skillet with snapper fillets. Return to heat and simmer for 5 to 10 minutes until heated through. Transfer snapper to dinner plates and top with sauce. Garnish with a sprig of parsley and serve.

Serve this snapper with fresh pasta, Spanish rice, or a baked potato, plus green beans amandine or a sautéed julienne medley of squash, carrots, and red bell peppers.

Serves 4

OLD SAN FRANCISCO STEAK & SEAFOOD HOUSE
10223 Sahara
San Antonio, Texas 78216
(210) 342-2321

◪ Pecan-Crusted Chicken and Dijon White Wine Sauce

8 boneless, skinless chicken
   breast halves
1 cup bread crumbs
1/4 cup finely minced pecan
   pieces
1 cup all-purpose flour
2 eggs beaten with 2
   tablespoons water
1/4 cup olive oil
1 cup dry white wine
1 cup heavy cream
1/4 cup Dijon mustard
Salt and pepper to taste
Worcestershire sauce
   (optional)
Chopped fresh parsley

In a shallow bowl, mix bread crumbs and pecans thoroughly. Dredge each chicken breast in flour, then dip into beaten egg mixture, then coat with bread crumb–pecan mix. Refrigerate for 30 minutes so pecans will stick better to chicken.

Preheat oven to 350 degrees. In a skillet, sauté chicken breasts in olive oil until golden brown on each side. Finish by baking for 10 to 15 minutes.

Heat wine in a saucepan and reduce by half, then add cream and reduce by a third. Add mustard and simmer until consistency becomes sauce-like. Season with salt and pepper and Worcestershire, if desired.

Cut each chicken breast into strips, lay the strips on a serving plate, and top with sauce. Garnish with chopped parsley and serve.

Dijon mustard adds a special zip to this creamy sauce.

Serves 4 to 8

CAFE CAMILLE
517 East Woodlawn
San Antonio, Texas 78212
(210) 735-2307

ꙮ Grilled Southwest Chicken with Jalapeño Butter

6 (7- to 8-ounce) boneless,
  skinless chicken breasts
1 cup Italian salad dressing
1/4 cup jalapeño jelly, melted

In a glass baking dish or large resealable plastic bag, combine chicken breasts and Italian dressing, and marinate overnight in refrigerator.

Remove breasts from marinade and place on prepared grill. Baste with jalapeño jelly while grilling. When breasts are cooked through (about 5 to 8 minutes per side), transfer to dinner plates and top each with a pat of **Jalapeño Butter**, letting it melt slightly before serving.

Pour the remainder of the jar of jalapeño jelly over a large block of cream cheese and serve as an appetizer with crackers.

Serves 6

Jalapeño Butter

1 fresh jalapeño chili
2 tablespoons chopped red
  bell pepper
1 clove garlic
1 parsley sprig
1/2 teaspoon Worcestershire
  sauce
1/8 teaspoon Tabasco sauce
1/2 teaspoon paprika
1/2 teaspoon cayenne pepper
1/2 cup (1 stick) butter, room
  temperature

Remove stem and seeds from jalapeño and discard. Place jalapeño in a food processor fitted with a metal blade and whirl with bell pepper, garlic, parsley, Worcestershire, Tabasco, paprika, and cayenne until peppers are finely minced. Add softened butter to mixture and process until spices and peppers are completely incorporated (stop as necessary to scrape down sides with a rubber spatula). Remove butter from bowl and, using plastic wrap, form into a roll about 1-1/2 inches in diameter. Freeze (up to a month) and slice as needed.

Makes about 3/4 cup

CAPPY'S RESTAURANT
5011 Broadway
San Antonio, Texas 78209
(210) 828-9669

Chicken Breast Roll-Ups

8 boneless, skinless chicken
   breast halves
1/2 cup melted butter or
   margarine
1 large clove garlic, minced
1-1/2 cups toasted croutons,
   crushed finely
1/3 cup grated Parmesan
   cheese
1-1/2 teaspoons chopped fresh
   parsley
Salt and pepper to taste
1 tablespoon paprika
Juice of 1 lemon

With a meat cleaver or mallet, pound chicken breasts to 1/4-inch thickness and set aside.

Combine butter or margarine with garlic in a shallow bowl, stirring well. Set aside.

Preheat oven to 350 degrees. Combine croutons, cheese, parsley, salt, pepper, and paprika in a large shallow bowl. Dip each chicken breast into the garlic butter and then into crouton mixture to coat. Roll up each breast, secure with a toothpick if necessary, and then lay seam-side down in a lightly greased baking pan. Squeeze lemon juice over rolled breasts. Bake for about 35 to 45 minutes, until chicken is done. Remove toothpicks before serving.

This makes a delicious entree served with steamed broccoli and fresh fruit, or slice the roll-ups into rounds and serve as an appetizer. The recipe can made up to 12 hours in advance, then covered with plastic wrap and refrigerated.

Serves 4 to 8

ARLENE'S CAFE
426 Seventh Street
Comfort, Texas 78013
(210) 995-3330

⟑ Pollo alla Sorrentina

2 (6-ounce) boneless, skinless
  chicken breasts
Salt and pepper to taste
All-purpose flour
1 tablespoon olive oil
6 mushrooms, sliced
1/2 teaspoon minced garlic
1/3 teaspoon dried oregano
  leaves
1/3 teaspoon dried sage
1 cup dry white wine
1 tablespoon melted butter
  combined with 2 teaspoons
  all-purpose flour
2 (3/4-ounce) slices mozzarella
  cheese

Sprinkle chicken breasts with salt and pepper, then dust with flour. Heat olive oil in a sauté pan until hot, then add chicken and brown. Turn and brown the other sides, then stir in mushrooms and sauté with chicken.

When chicken is almost done, drain off olive oil and add garlic, oregano, sage, salt, and pepper. Pour in wine and cook for about 4 to 5 minutes. Remove chicken and reduce sauce by a third to a half. Thicken sauce by whisking in flour-butter combination, then return chicken to sauce. Top chicken with mozzarella slices, cover pan, and cook for 30 seconds to melt cheese. Serve chicken topped with sauce.

A side of pasta tossed with garlic butter accompanies this chicken nicely. Fresh sage makes the dish even more special; increase to 1 teaspoon if using the fresh herb.

Serves 2

BOCCACCIO RISTORANTE ITALIANO
205 North Presa Street
San Antonio, Texas 78205
(210) 225-1500

⚜ Salpicón of Texas Mesquite-Grilled Chicken

1 pound boneless, skinless chicken breasts, grilled over mesquite and diced
1 teaspoon minced fresh epazote or marjoram
1 tablespoon rice vinegar
1 teaspoon sugar
1 tablespoon fresh lime juice
2 tablespoons minced shallots or sweet onions, rinsed under hot water
2 tablespoons extra-virgin olive oil
1/4 cup diced red bell pepper
2 tablespoons minced serrano chilies
1 avocado, peeled and sliced

In a nonmetallic bowl, combine epazote, vinegar, sugar, lime juice, shallots, oil, peppers, and chilies. Mix well, then add chicken and toss. Serve garnished with avocado slices.

This is a Texas interpretation of salpicón, *a savory mixture of cooked, diced ingredients. It is delicious served atop a bed of greens, as a filling for* bolillos, *or as part of a salad buffet. Refrigerated, it keeps well for several days.*

Serves 4

STETSON RESTAURANT
Hilton Palacio del Rio Hotel
200 South Alamo Street
San Antonio, Texas 78205
(210) 222-1400

✿ Chicken with Artichoke Hearts and Sherry

1 pound boneless, skinless chicken breasts, cut into 1-1/2-inch pieces

1/2 cup all-purpose flour seasoned with 1/2 teaspoon salt and 1/4 teaspoon pepper

2 tablespoons Spanish extra-virgin olive oil

3 cloves garlic, crushed

1/2 teaspoon freshly ground pepper

1 (14-ounce) can artichoke hearts, drained (10 to 12 hearts)

3/4 cup Oloroso-style sherry (sweet, rich, and full-flavored)

1/2 cup (1 stick) butter, cut into small pieces

1 tablespoon chopped parsley

With a meat mallet, pound each piece of chicken to an even thickness of 1/4 inch. Dredge in seasoned flour and set aside.

Heat olive oil in a large sauté pan, then add garlic and pepper and cook for 30 seconds. Add chicken pieces and sauté for 1 to 2 minutes, then turn each piece. Add artichoke hearts.

Carefully pour sherry into pan, standing back in case alcohol ignites. Cook for 1 minute to evaporate the alcohol, then add butter to enrich sauce and thicken it slightly. Add parsley, then allow sauce to simmer and reduce slightly.

Try this dish with saffron-flavored rice and a fresh vegetable medley.

Serves 4

BARCELONA'S MEDITERRANEAN CAFE
4901 Broadway, Suite 120
San Antonio, Texas 78209
(210) 822-6129

President Grant's Chicken

4 (4-ounce) boneless, skinless
　　chicken breast halves,
　　pounded thin
1 cup small mushrooms, sliced
4 teaspoons plus 2 tablespoons
　　unsalted butter
1 medium clove garlic, minced
1/2 cup chopped onion
1/2 cup dry red wine
1/4 cup all-purpose flour
1/2 cup dry white wine
1 cup heavy cream
1 teaspoon dried thyme
Salt and pepper to taste

Preheat oven to 350 degrees. In a medium skillet, sauté half the mushrooms in 2 teaspoons butter until nearly tender. Add half the garlic and the onions and cook until tender. Add red wine and simmer until reduced by half. Divide mushroom mixture among 4 chicken breasts, spooning it into the center of each. Roll chicken breasts up tightly, using a toothpick to hold each breast together. Lightly dust breasts with flour and sauté in 2 tablespoons melted butter until brown on all sides. Finish chicken in the oven, baking for about 10 minutes or until done.

While chicken is baking, in a small skillet sauté remaining mushrooms and garlic in remaining 2 teaspoons butter. Add white wine and simmer to reduce by half. Add cream and reduce again by half. Stir in thyme, salt, and pepper. Serve rolled breasts whole or sliced on the diagonal, topped with sauce.

This dish is named after President Grant, who stayed at the Menger Hotel. Fettuccine, cooked al dente and topped with some of the cream sauce, makes an excellent side dish for this entree.

Serves 4

THE COLONIAL ROOM RESTAURANT
The Menger Hotel
204 Alamo Plaza
San Antonio, Texas 78205
(210) 223-4361

Rock-Charred Lamb and Eggplant Brochettes on Rosemary Skewers

1-1/2 pounds lean boneless lamb (leg or shoulder), cut into 1-inch cubes
1/4 cup balsamic vinegar
5 cloves garlic
2 tablespoons chopped mixed fresh herbs, such as basil, thyme, oregano, or marjoram
1 teaspoon kosher salt
1/2 teaspoon coarsely cracked pepper
1/4 cup plus 2 tablespoons olive oil
1 red onion, cut into 1-inch wedges
1 red bell pepper, cut into 1-inch pieces
1 yellow bell pepper, cut into 1-inch pieces
4–6 stalks fresh rosemary, each about 10 inches long
1 eggplant

In a blender or food processor, combine vinegar, garlic, mixed herbs, salt, and pepper, and whirl until smooth. With machine running, slowly drizzle in oil. Pour mixture into a nonmetallic bowl or a large resealable plastic bag, add lamb, onion, and bell peppers, and marinate in refrigerator for 4 hours or overnight.

Prepare rosemary skewers by stripping off all leaves except about 1 inch on the end for a garnish. Sharpen the other end a little to make skewering easier. (You can substitute bamboo skewers, soaked first in water for 10 minutes.)

Remove lamb and vegetables from marinade and reserve liquid. Peel eggplant and halve lengthwise. Cut long, thin slices about 1/4-inch thick and brush them well on both sides with reserved marinade. Skewer lamb and vegetables onto rosemary branches, weaving long eggplant slices back and forth between each cube (use about 2 slices of eggplant per skewer). Brochettes can be cooked on a "Hot Rock" cooking stone, on a barbecue grill, or under the broiler. (Be careful not to overcook; lamb is best cooked medium-rare or medium.)

Serve these brochettes on a bed of sautéed or wilted spinach with lemon, and hot rice or barley pilaf. Rosemary stalks are also attractive as skewers for shrimp.

Serves 4 to 6

THE ANAQUA GRILL
Plaza San Antonio Hotel
555 South Alamo Street
San Antonio, Texas 78205
(210) 229-1000

⚑ Spicy Lamb Brochette

2 pounds lamb tenders (or
  boned leg of lamb), cut into
  1-inch cubes
1 cup Spanish extra-virgin
  olive oil
2 tablespoons chopped garlic
1/4 cup chopped parsley
1 teaspoon salt
1 teaspoon pepper
1 teaspoon crushed red pepper
  flakes
1 teaspoon dried oregano
1 teaspoon ground cumin
1 teaspoon paprika
Chopped parsley and rosemary
  sprigs

In a large bowl, combine olive oil, garlic, parsley, salt, pepper, red pepper flakes, oregano, cumin, and paprika. Add lamb cubes, cover, and marinate in the refrigerator for at least 12 hours.

Place lamb cubes on metal or bamboo skewers (soak bamboo skewers in water to prevent burning) and grill or broil to desired doneness (about 15 minutes). Serve on a platter, each brochette garnished with chopped parsley and a rosemary sprig.

These are excellent served over couscous or rice pilaf. A yogurt dill sauce also offers a nice accompaniment.

Serves 4 to 6

BARCELONA'S MEDITERRANEAN CAFE
4901 Broadway, Suite 120
San Antonio, Texas 78209
(210) 822-6129

⬚ Tenderloins Fiesta

1/2 pound beef tenderloin or
    filet mignon, cut into
    1/2-inch cubes
2 tablespoons olive oil
1 tablespoon minced green
    onion (white and green
    parts)
5 large mushrooms, sliced
2 fresh jalapeño chilies, seeded
    and sliced very thin
1 teaspoon Dijon mustard
1 tablespoon minced cilantro
1/2 teaspoon minced garlic
1 cup brown sauce (or a
    1.2-ounce package Knorr
    demi-glace sauce mix,
    prepared as directed)
Salt and pepper to taste

Heat oil in a sauté pan and brown meat on both sides, about 1 minute per side. Stir in onion and mushrooms, sautéing for about 2 minutes, then add jalapeños. Sauté for 1 minute, then stir in remaining ingredients. Cook for 2 to 3 minutes more, then remove from heat and serve.

Ruffino's serves this flavorful beef dish over saffron rice, but it's also delicious over noodles or pasta.

Serves 2

RUFFINO'S RESTAURANT & BAR
9802 Colonnade
San Antonio, Texas 78230
(210) 641-6100

⚵Tochocan

1 pound beef tenderloin tips
   or sirloin, cut into 1/2-inch
   pieces
Juice of 1 lime
Salt and freshly ground pepper
   to taste
4 thick slices bacon
1/2 pound (2 links) top-quality
   chorizo (Mexican sausage)

In a nonmetallic bowl or a resealable plastic bag, marinate beef with lime juice, salt, and pepper in refrigerator for 2 hours.

In a heavy skillet, cook bacon and chorizo until bacon is crisp and chorizo is done (break up chorizo as it cooks). Remove bacon and chop. Drain fat completely from skillet containing chorizo. Add beef tenderloin, marinade liquid, and chopped bacon to chorizo and cook for about 5 minutes.

This is one of the most popular beef dishes at La Calesa. Serve it with warm flour tortillas, black beans, rice, and plenty of fresh salsa.

Serves 4

LA CALESA
2103 East Hildebrand
San Antonio, Texas 78209
(210) 822-4475

❧ Grilled Round Steaks with Chimichurri Sauce

6 (5- to 6-ounce) pieces inside
    beef round, cut 1/4-inch
    thick
1/4 cup olive oil
Salt and pepper to taste

A day before serving, prepare **Chimichurri Sauce** and refrigerate. (Bring to room temperature before serving.)

Flatten meat with a mallet to 1/8-inch thickness. Brush with olive oil on each side and season with salt and pepper. Grill quickly over medium-hot coals, no more than 1 minute per side. Cover with **Chimichurri Sauce** and serve.

This recipe has its origins in Argentina. It is important to pound the meat thoroughly before grilling to completely tenderize it.

Serves 6

Chimichurri Sauce

6–8 jalapeño chilies, seeded
    and diced
1 cup diced yellow onion
8 cloves garlic, pressed
1/2 cup finely chopped parsley
1 tablespoon dried oregano
    leaves
3/4–1 tablespoon crushed
    peppercorns
1 cup olive oil
1/2 cup balsamic vinegar
1/2 cup fresh lime juice
1/4 cup water
1-1/2 teaspoons sugar

Combine all ingredients in a tightly covered container and refrigerate for at least 24 hours before serving.

Leftover sauce keeps well for at least 10 days in the refrigerator. Try it with other meats or as a dip for corn chips.

Makes about 3 cups

ZUNI GRILL
511 East Riverwalk
San Antonio, Texas 78205
(210) 227-0864

⛧Arlene's Favorite Pot Roast

1 large beef chuck roast (about
  6 pounds)
1 teaspoon onion powder
1 teaspoon garlic powder or
  granulated garlic
Pepper to taste
Cajun seasoning to taste
All-purpose flour
2 (10-1/2-ounce) cans
  condensed golden
  mushroom soup, undiluted
  (no substitutions)
2 envelopes dry onion soup
  mix
3–4 soup cans of water
2 tablespoons Worcestershire
  sauce
1 tablespoon A-1 Steak Sauce

Preheat oven to 450 degrees. Sprinkle roast with onion powder, garlic powder, pepper, and Cajun seasoning, then sprinkle with flour to lightly coat. Place in a large Dutch oven and bake, covered, for 40 minutes. While roast is cooking, combine remaining ingredients in a large bowl and stir to mix well.

Reduce oven temperature to 250 degrees and remove roast from oven. Pour liquid mixture over meat, then cover and return to oven. Bake for about 6 hours (or longer, depending on size of roast), until meat is tender. Serve roast warm in its own gravy.

This roast can be fully prepared a day in advance of serving. Cool to room temperature, then refrigerate overnight. Reheat before serving.

Serves 12 to 16

ARLENE'S CAFE
426 Seventh Street
Comfort, Texas 78013
(210) 995-3330

☗ Gini's Meatloaf

1-1/4 pounds lean ground beef
  or turkey
1/3 cup packed chopped
  parsley
1 small onion, finely minced
1 small carrot, finely minced
1/2 teaspoon freshly ground
  pepper
1 teaspoon sea salt
1/4 teaspoon garlic powder
1/2 cup ketchup
1 egg
2 cups fresh whole wheat
  bread crumbs

Preheat oven to 350 degrees. In a large mixing bowl, combine meat, parsley, onion, carrot, pepper, salt, and garlic powder until well blended. Add ketchup and egg and mix well, followed by bread crumbs. Mix well.

Divide mixture into 6 to 8 equal portions and place on a baking sheet with sides, or press all into a 10-by-3-by-3-inch loaf pan. Bake individual loaves for 45 minutes, or single whole loaf for 60 to 90 minutes.

This meatloaf is so succulent, you'll forget how healthful it is for you. The leftovers make great sandwiches!

Serves 6 to 8

GINI'S HOME COOKING & BAKERY
7214 Blanco Road
San Antonio, Texas 78216
(210) 342-2768

⚜ Crosswalk Chili with Pinto Beans

3 medium onions, chopped
3 cloves garlic, minced
1 large green bell pepper, chopped
2 tablespoons vegetable oil
2 pounds chili-grind beef (or ground beef)
1 teaspoon ground cumin
1 teaspoon dried oregano
1/4 teaspoon cayenne pepper, or to taste
1/2 cup chili powder
Mrs. Dash or salt to taste
Pepper to taste
1 serrano chili, seeded and minced
1 (28-ounce) can whole peeled tomatoes with liquid
1 (8-ounce) can tomato sauce
1 cup water
1 pound pinto beans, cooked (reserve cooking liquid)

Place onions, garlic, and bell pepper in an 8-quart stockpot with vegetable oil. Sauté over medium heat for 5 to 10 minutes. Add chili meat and stir occasionally for 15 minutes or until meat is browned. While meat is browning, stir in cumin, oregano, cayenne pepper, chili powder, Mrs. Dash, pepper, and serrano chili. When meat is browned, lower heat to a simmer.

Chop tomatoes in a blender or food processor and add to pot along with tomato sauce and water. Let simmer, stirring occasionally, for at least 1 hour. Add pinto beans to mixture, adding a little cooking liquid from the beans to bring chili to desired thickness.

Try this topped with grated cheese and chopped onions. Or, to create a Texas favorite, pour the chili over corn chips and top it with grated cheddar cheese to make "Frito pie."

Serves 8 to 12

CROSSWALK DELI
121-C Alamo Plaza
San Antonio, Texas 78205
(210) 228-0880

⛊ Albondigas with Chipotle Sauce

1/4 teaspoon dried thyme
1/4 teaspoon dried marjoram
1 small bay leaf
1/4 teaspoon cumin seed
8 peppercorns
2 teaspoons salt
1/3 cup milk
1 raw egg, plus 1 hard-cooked
  egg, chopped finely
2 cloves garlic
1 slice stale bread
1/3 cup partially cooked white
  rice
3/4 pound ground beef
3/4 pound ground pork

Prepare **Chipotle Sauce** and set aside.

In a blender or food processor, combine thyme, marjoram, bay leaf, cumin, peppercorns, salt, milk, raw egg, and garlic, and whirl until smooth. Soak bread in this mixture until it becomes mushy, then combine it with rice, ground beef, ground pork, and hard-cooked egg. Work mixture well with your hands, then form it into 24 meatballs about 1-1/2 inches in diameter.

Add meatballs to **Chipotle Sauce**, cover pan, and simmer over medium-low heat for about 45 minutes, turning meatballs occasionally. Remove from heat when meatballs are cooked through and spongy.

These meatballs are a specialty of Mexico and one of Teka Molino's most popular offerings.

Serves 6

Chipotle Sauce

6 dry chipotle chilies
2 tablespoons vegetable oil
1-1/2 pounds ripe tomatoes,
    broiled and cored
1/2 medium white onion,
    sliced thinly
2 cloves garlic
1/4 teaspoon cumin seed
1/2 teaspoon salt, or to taste
2 tablespoons water
2-1/2 cups beef broth

Toast chilies on a hot griddle, turning occasionally, until they become soft and flexible. Slit chilies and remove seeds and veins. Heat oil and sauté chilies until they turn very dark brown. Reserve oil and transfer chilies along with broiled tomatoes to a blender or food processor and whirl until smooth.

Reheat reserved cooking oil in pan and sauté onion until translucent and soft. Crush garlic, cumin, and salt together using either a chef's knife on a cutting board or a mortar and pestle. Combine mixture with water and add to onions. Fry over high heat, stirring continually, until almost dry, then add chili-tomato mixture, stirring constantly, until sauce is reduced and thickened. Stir broth into sauce and remove from heat.

Makes about 4 cups

TEKA MOLINO
7231 San Pedro
San Antonio, Texas 78216
(210) 344-7281
2403 North St. Mary's Street
San Antonio, Texas 78212
(210) 735-5471

⚑ Italian Sausage Roll

4 (4-inch) links mild Italian
  sausage
1 cup water
3 tablespoons plus 1 teaspoon
  olive oil
1 medium onion, sliced into
  rings
1 green bell pepper, cut into
  long, thin strips
1 red bell pepper, cut into
  long, thin strips
1 heaping teaspoon dry yeast
1 teaspoon sugar
1-1/2 cups bread flour
1/2 teaspoon salt
2 cups grated mozzarella
  cheese
2 cups marinara or spaghetti
  sauce, purchased or
  prepared

Preheat oven to 350 degrees. Place sausage links in an ovenproof container with 1/2 cup water. Roast, uncovered, for 30 to 45 minutes or until done. When cool, quarter each sausage lengthwise and set aside.

In a heavy skillet, heat 3 tablespoons olive oil. Add onion and peppers and sauté over medium heat for about 2 minutes. Reduce heat to low and cook, covered, for 10 minutes, stirring occasionally. Set aside.

Heat remaining 1/2 cup water to 105 to 115 degrees and pour into a bowl. Sprinkle yeast over water and stir until dissolved. Mix in sugar, flour, salt, and 1 teaspoon olive oil. Knead dough on a lightly floured surface until elastic. Shape into a ball, place in a greased bowl, and turn ball over to grease top of dough. Cover and let rise in a draft-free place for 1 hour. Punch dough down and knead slightly. Wrap dough in plastic wrap and refrigerate for 1 hour.

Preheat oven to 400 degrees. Punch dough down, then roll out into a 14-inch circle. Cut dough into 4 wedge-shaped pieces. Place 4 slices of sausage at the wide end of each wedge, then add a fourth of the onion mixture and 1/2 cup cheese. Starting at the wide end, roll each wedge up to form a crescent. Bake for about 15 minutes or until golden brown. Serve hot with warm marinara or spaghetti sauce.

As a variation, try serving these rolls with Ranch dressing instead of or with the marinara sauce.

Serves 4

**VILLA ITALIAN
SPECIALTIES**
910 North Star Mall
San Antonio, Texas 78216
(210) 342-3428

Rosemary–Red Serrano Roasted Pork Loin

1 (3-pound) center-cut pork
loin roast
1/4 cup soy sauce
1/2 cup chopped fresh
rosemary
8 red serrano chilies
(substitute green if red not
available)
1/4 cup minced garlic
3 tablespoons cracked pepper
1/4 cup peanut oil
1/2 cup fine bread crumbs,
made from toasted bread
Salt to taste

Preheat oven to 350 degrees. In a blender or food processor, combine soy sauce, rosemary, serrano chilies, garlic, and pepper. After blending well, slowly add oil, followed by bread crumbs. Set resulting paste aside.

Salt pork loin, then pack rosemary-serrano paste evenly onto all sides of roast. Roast pork until it registers 160 degrees internally (about 50 minutes). Cut into 1/2- to 3/4-inch slices and serve.

Accompany this full-flavored roast with mashed potatoes and a chipotle demi-glace, if desired.

Serves 8

CASCABEL RESTAURANT
Sheraton Fiesta Hotel
37 Northeast Loop 410
San Antonio, Texas 78216
(210) 366-2424

⚲ Smokehouse Special

1/4 cup mayonnaise
4 pieces lightly toasted bread
16 slices smoked bacon,
   cooked until crisp and
   drained
8 slices tomato
8 raw onion rings
8 (1-ounce) slices cheddar
   cheese
2 jalapeño chilies, sliced

Preheat oven to 400 degrees. Spread 1 tablespoon mayonnaise on one side of each piece of bread and then top each with the following ingredients, in order: 4 slices bacon, 2 slices tomato, 2 onion rings, 2 slices cheese, and several jalapeño slices. Transfer topped bread to a baking sheet and bake until cheese is well melted (8 to 10 minutes).

These are delicious served with potato salad or fresh fruit.

Serves 4

NEW BRAUNFELS SMOKEHOUSE
6450 North New Braunfels
San Antonio, Texas 78209
(210) 826-6008
140 Highway 46 South
New Braunfels, Texas 78130
(210) 625-2416

Sweet Endings

◉ Coconut Sorbet

3 (13-1/2-ounce) cans coconut
   milk (not cream of coconut)
1 cup water
1 cup sugar
Dash of salt
Chopped peanuts

Combine coconut milk, water, sugar, and salt in a bowl, then pour mixture into the chilled can of an ice cream maker. Follow manufacturer's directions for making sorbet. Store in the freezer. Remove from freezer 10 minutes before serving and scoop sorbet into individual dishes. Top with chopped peanuts.

It's hard to believe anything this simple can be so good. This sorbet was selected as one of the best signature dishes in San Antonio by the San Antonio Express-News *"Food & Wine" section.*

Makes 1 generous quart

THAI KITCHEN
445 McCarty
San Antonio, Texas 78216
(210) 344-8366

◉ White Chocolate and Pistachio Ice Cream

6 egg yolks
1-1/2 cups sugar
1/4 cup cornstarch
1 teaspoon vanilla extract
1 quart half-and-half
8 ounces white chocolate,
 shaved
3/4 cup toasted pistachios,
 chopped coarsely

Beat egg yolks, sugar, cornstarch, and vanilla in a stainless steel bowl until well blended and pale yellow. Heat 2 cups half-and-half over medium heat almost to a boil. Slowly stir part of hot liquid into egg mixture until smooth, then add egg mixture to pot and cook over low heat until completely thickened (do not allow to boil). Stir chocolate shavings into mixture until completely melted. Add remaining cold half-and-half and blend well. Allow to cool completely.

Freeze in the chilled container of an ice cream maker, following manufacturer's directions. Add nuts about 10 minutes before ice cream is finished churning.

This is a great summer treat that can be made a month ahead. Just let the ice cream sit at room temperature for 5 minutes to soften it.

Makes 1-1/2 quarts

POLO'S AT THE FAIRMOUNT
401 South Alamo Street
San Antonio, Texas 78205
(210) 224-8800

◉ Fried Ice Cream with Kahlúa Hot Fudge Sauce

Vanilla ice cream
1 cup corn flakes
1 cup sweetened flaked
   coconut
1 cup firmly packed brown
   sugar
1 egg
2 tablespoons milk
Hot vegetable oil
Whipped cream and chocolate
   shavings

Scoop vanilla ice cream into 4 large balls, making sure scoops are well shaped. Freeze.

Preheat oven to 350 degrees. Crush corn flakes, combine in a bowl with coconut and brown sugar, and toast on a baking sheet for about 10 minutes or until golden (do not burn). In a separate bowl, combine egg and milk for an eggwash. Dip frozen ice cream scoops into eggwash and roll in corn flake mixture to coat well. Freeze scoops again.

Place coated scoops in a fry basket or strainer and dip into hot oil for 8 to 10 seconds. Remove immediately and serve topped with **Kahlúa Hot Fudge Sauce** and garnished with whipped cream and chocolate shavings.

This impressive dessert will win you raves from guests.

Serves 4

Kahlúa Hot Fudge Sauce

2 tablespoons Kahlúa liqueur
1 cup bottled hot fudge sauce

Combine liqueur and hot fudge sauce in the top of a double boiler and gently heat until hot, but not boiling. To reheat, do so in the double boiler.

Makes 1 cup

CACTUS FLOWER CAFE
Marriott Riverwalk Hotel
711 East Riverwalk
San Antonio, Texas 78205

❂ Biga's Gingered Rice Pudding with Dried Cherry Sauce

1 quart half-and-half
1 quart heavy cream, plus 2
   cups whipped firm
1 cup uncooked long-grain
   white rice
1 cup sugar
1 (2-inch) piece unpeeled
   fresh ginger, sliced into a fan
1/2 vanilla bean, split
Pinch of kosher salt
5 egg yolks

Combine first 7 ingredients (except whipped cream) in a heavy-bottomed saucepan. Bring to a boil, then simmer uncovered until mixture becomes thick (at least 1 hour). Stir often, using a wooden spoon to prevent sticking.

When the mixture is thick, remove from heat and discard ginger and vanilla bean. Beat egg yolks. Stir a small amount of hot mixture into beaten yolks, then add yolk mixture to pan and stir in well. Cool in refrigerator, stirring occasionally. When completely cool, gradually fold in whipped cream (thickness is determined by amount of cream added). If too runny, spoon into cups and glaze under broiler until brown. Serve topped with **Dried Cherry Sauce.**

This bears little resemblance to the rice pudding we grew up with!

Serves 12

Dried Cherry Sauce

2 cups dried cherries (available
   at specialty store)
2 cups apple cider
2 teaspoons fresh lemon juice
1 cup sugar
1/8 teaspoon ground cinnamon
1/8 teaspoon ground cloves
1/2 cup pecan halves

Combine cherries, cider, and lemon juice in a saucepan. Cover and simmer until cherries are soft (about 10 minutes). Add sugar, cinnamon, and cloves, and slowly bring to a boil, stirring occasionally. Boil for about 10 minutes, stirring often. Add nuts during the last 3 minutes of cooking. Remove from heat and serve at room temperature.

Makes about 3 cups

RESTAURANT BIGA
206 East Locust Street
San Antonio, Texas 78212
(210) 225-0722

◙ Ruth's Chris Bread Pudding

1-1/4 cups sugar
1/2 cup firmly packed light
  brown sugar
1/8 teaspoon ground nutmeg
1-1/2 teaspoons ground
  cinnamon
6 beaten eggs
1 tablespoon vanilla extract
1 tablespoon bourbon
Pinch of salt
2 cups milk
1 pint half-and-half
1/2 cup (1 stick) unsalted
  butter
1/2 cup raisins
1/2 apple, peeled, cored, and
  diced
1/2 pound French bread, cut
  into 1/2-inch cubes and
  toasted
Vanilla ice cream

Preheat oven to 350 degrees. Combine sugars and divide in half. Add nutmeg, cinnamon, eggs, vanilla, bourbon, and salt to one of the sugar mixtures. In a saucepan, combine milk, half-and-half, and butter with other sugar mixture. Bring to a boil, then remove from heat.

Whisk a small amount of hot mixture into egg mixture, then add egg mixture along with raisins and apples to heated mixture. Add toasted bread cubes and let stand until soaked through to the center.

Pour mixture into 2 buttered 10-by-3-by-3-inch loaf pans or 1 buttered 9-by-13-inch pan. Bake until just set (about 30 to 45 minutes), then serve warm with vanilla ice cream.

This fragrant bread pudding needs no additional sauce, as generous amounts of butter, half-and-half, and spices make it moist and flavorful.

Serves 12 to 16

RUTH'S CHRIS STEAK HOUSE
7720 Jones-Maltsberger, Suite 118
San Antonio, Texas 78216
(210) 821-5051

◉ Flan Heroico

3/4 cup sugar
2 (8-ounce) packages cream
    cheese, room temperature
1 (14-ounce) can sweetened
    condensed milk
2 cups milk
4 eggs
2 teaspoons vanilla extract

Preheat oven to 350 degrees. Place sugar in a hot skillet and cook until caramel colored. Quickly pour caramel into a 2-quart round glass baking dish. Swirl caramel around quickly to cover bottom and sides of dish, then set aside.

Beat cream cheese until smooth, then beat in condensed milk. In a separate bowl, beat milk with eggs and vanilla, then combine with cheese mixture and mix well. Pour mixture into caramel-coated baking dish. Place dish inside a larger pan and add 1-1/2 to 2 inches of hot water to outer pan. Bake until firm (about 1 hour). When set, loosen custard from sides of dish and tilt dish to allow melted caramel to cover sides. Chill for 4 to 6 hours, then invert onto a plate, cut into wedges, and serve.

This ultra-rich dessert has a consistency more like a cheesecake than a traditional flan.

Serves 10

THE ORIGINAL MEXICAN RESTAURANT
528 Riverwalk
San Antonio, Texas 78205
(210) 224-9951

⬢ Apple Crepia with Calvados Sauce

2 sheets frozen puff pastry,
    thawed for 30 minutes
2 egg yolks
4 Granny Smith apples,
    peeled, cored, and sliced
    thinly (hold in a bowl of cool
    water mixed with 1 teaspoon
    lemon juice)
1/4 cup sugar
Powdered sugar

Preheat oven to 425 degrees. Roll out puff pastry to approximately 1/4-inch thickness. Using a salad plate as a guide, cut four 6-inch circles from puff pastry. Place circles on a baking sheet with sides and brush with beaten egg yolks.

Arrange apples on pastry, overlapping slices slightly, starting at outer edge. Sprinkle 1 tablespoon sugar over each pastry, taking care not to spill sugar on baking sheet. Bake for 12 to 15 minutes, or until golden brown. Arrange on a serving plate, spooning **Calvados Sauce** around each pastry and topping each with a sprinkling of powdered sugar.

If desired, additional chopped fruit can be spooned onto the sauce for variance of color and flavor.

Serves 4

Calvados Sauce

1/4 cup sugar
3 egg yolks
1/4 cup heavy cream
3/4 cup half-and-half
2–4 tablespoons Calvados
    brandy

In a bowl beat together sugar and egg yolks. Combine cream and half-and-half in a saucepan and bring to a boil, then whisk slowly into sugar and eggs. Return mixture to pan and stir over low heat until mixture coats and leaves a path on the back of a wooden spoon. Strain sauce through a sieve and cool. Just before serving, add Calvados and stir.

Makes 1 cup

L'ETOILE
6106 Broadway
San Antonio, Texas 78209
(210) 826-4551

◎ Chocolate Fudge Pecan Pie

4 eggs, beaten with a whisk
2 cups sugar
3 tablespoons melted butter
3 (1-ounce) squares
   unsweetened chocolate,
   melted
1/8 teaspoon salt
1/4 teaspoon fresh lemon juice
1 cup chopped pecans
1 (9-inch) unbaked pie shell
Vanilla ice cream

Preheat oven to 350 degrees. In a mixing bowl, blend together eggs, sugar, butter, chocolate, salt, and lemon juice. Sprinkle pecans in the bottom of pie shell, then pour egg mixture over pecans. Bake for about 40 minutes (pie should be set but slightly shaky in the middle; it will thicken as it cools). Cool completely, then serve with ice cream.

You'll be delighted by this rich dessert. When topped with ice cream, the taste resembles a decadent hot fudge sundae.

APPLE ANNIE'S TEA ROOM & BAKERY
555 Bitters Road
San Antonio, Texas 78216
(210) 491-0226

❂ Derby Pie with Bourbon Whipped Cream

1-1/2 cups sugar
1/4 cup plus 2 tablespoons
  all-purpose flour
3 eggs, beaten
3/4 cup (1-1/2 sticks) butter,
  melted or at room
  temperature
1-1/2 cups chopped walnuts or
  pecans
1-1/2 cups semisweet
  chocolate chips
3 tablespoons bourbon
1 (10-inch) unbaked pie shell

Preheat oven to 350 degrees. In a mixing bowl, combine sugar, flour, and eggs. Add butter and mix, followed by nuts, chocolate chips, and bourbon. Pour mixture into unbaked pie shell and bake for 30 to 35 minutes, until pie is done and set in the center. Cool completely, then serve topped with **Bourbon Whipped Cream.**

This rich, luscious pie is worth every one of its calories. Prepare it for any occasion when you want to impress.

Serves 8

Bourbon Whipped Cream

1 cup heavy cream
2 tablespoons sugar
2 tablespoons bourbon

In a mixing bowl, whip the cream just until it starts to thicken. Add sugar and bourbon and whip until stiff.

Prepare this just before serving for the best flavor and texture.

THE COPPER KITCHEN
The Southwest Craft Center
300 Augusta
San Antonio, Texas 78205
(210) 224-0123

⦿ Texas Lime Chess Pie with Chantilly Cream

1 cup all-purpose flour
3/4 cup (1-1/2 sticks) butter, melted
1/4 cup powdered sugar
1/2 cup chopped pecans
1-1/2 cups sugar
1 tablespoon yellow cornmeal
1 tablespoon grated lime zest
1/4 cup milk
1/4 cup fresh lime juice
4 eggs

Preheat oven to 350 degrees. Combine flour, 1/2 cup melted butter, powdered sugar, and pecans, and press with your hands into a greased and floured 10-inch pie pan (take crust mixture completely up the sides of the pan). Bake until golden (about 15 minutes), then set aside and let cool completely.

Increase oven heat to 375 degrees. In a large bowl, combine remaining 1/4 cup melted butter, sugar, cornmeal, lime zest, milk, lime juice, and eggs, and beat together well with a whisk. Pour filling into cooled shell, then bake until pie is set (about 30 minutes). Remove from oven, cool at room temperature for 30 minutes, then refrigerate for 2 to 3 hours. Serve topped with **Chantilly Cream.**

This is one of Boudro's best-loved desserts. If there's too much filling for the pie shell, bake the extra in a small custard cup.

Serves 6 to 8

Chantilly Cream

1 cup heavy cream, well chilled
1/2 teaspoon vanilla extract
1 tablespoon sifted powdered sugar

Combine all ingredients in a chilled mixing bowl and beat until peaks begin to form (do not overbeat).

Makes about 2 cups

BOUDRO'S: A TEXAS BISTRO ON THE RIVER WALK
421 East Commerce Street
San Antonio, Texas 78205
(210) 224-8484

◉ Peanut Butter Ice Cream Pie

1/2 package graham crackers, crushed fine

2 tablespoons plus 1 teaspoon sugar

2-1/2 tablespoons butter, room temperature

3 tablespoons Cointreau liqueur

3/4 cup plus 1 tablespoon crunchy peanut butter

1 quart vanilla ice cream, softened

Preheat oven to 350 degrees. Combine crushed graham crackers, sugar, and butter, and press into the bottom of a 9-inch cake pan. Bake for 6 to 9 minutes, then remove from oven, cool, and refrigerate.

In a large bowl, mix Cointreau with peanut butter, then fold ice cream into mixture. Spoon mixture into the cold cake pan and freeze for 24 hours before serving.

Serve this as is, or drizzle it with hot fudge sauce for a special treat.

Serves 8

BISTRO TIME
5137 Fredericksburg Road
San Antonio, Texas 78229
(210) 344-6626

◙ Old-Fashioned Vinegar Pie

4-1/2 tablespoons evaporated
    milk, room temperature
3 tablespoons white vinegar
3/4 cup (1-1/2 sticks)
    margarine, room
    temperature
2 cups minus 2 tablespoons
    sugar
2 teaspoons all-purpose flour
5 eggs, room temperature
1/2 teaspoon vanilla extract
1 (10-inch) unbaked pie shell
Freshly grated nutmeg

Preheat oven to 350 degrees. In a small bowl, combine evaporated milk and vinegar, then set aside.

Using an electric mixer, cream together margarine and sugar. Stir in flour and mix until blended. Add eggs, 1 at a time, and mix well after each addition. Add vanilla. Slowly pour vinegar mixture into creamy mixture, mixing only to combine (do not overmix; the mixture may look slightly curdled). Pour into unbaked pie shell and sprinkle with nutmeg. Bake for about 35 to 40 minutes (do not overbake; pie will firm up more as it cools). Let pie set for 1 hour before cutting.

This dessert, which comes from a very old recipe, tastes like an egg custard pie, only better. It freezes well and makes a great holiday dessert.

Serves 8 to 10

ARLENE'S CAFE
426 Seventh Street
Comfort, Texas 78013
(210) 995-3330

◉ Margarita Pie

2 tablespoons tequila
1 tablespoon orange curaçao
   liqueur
1 tablespoon blue curaçao
   liqueur
1/4 cup fresh lime juice
1 (14-ounce) can sweetened
   condensed milk
1 cup heavy cream
1 (9-inch) graham cracker pie
   crust

In a mixing bowl, combine tequila, orange curaçao, blue curaçao, lime juice, and sweetened condensed milk. In a separate bowl, whip heavy cream until stiff, then fold into tequila mixture. Pour filling into pie shell and place in the freezer. Serve when thoroughly frozen.

This pie also has an excellent flavor and texture when refrigerated rather than frozen.

Serves 6 to 8

ALAMO CAFE
9714 San Pedro
San Antonio, Texas 78216
(210) 341-4526
10060 Interstate 10 West
San Antonio, Texas 78230
(210) 691-8827

◙ Caramel Pecan Tart with Cream Cheese Frosting

1 cup plus 2–3 tablespoons heavy cream
1/4 cup plus 1 tablespoon butter
2 tablespoons light corn syrup
1 cup sugar
1/2 cup chopped pecans, walnuts, or macadamia nuts, plus additional to garnish
4 ounces semisweet chocolate chips or chopped chocolate, plus 4 ounces melted

Prepare **Tart Shell** and set aside to cool.

Pour 1/2 cup cream in a heavy-bottomed saucepan, add 1/4 cup butter, and heat gently until butter melts. Mix well and set aside.

In another heavy-bottomed pan, mix corn syrup and sugar, and heat over medium-high heat, stirring occasionally, until mixture is caramel colored (do not overcook). Slowly pour warm cream mixture into corn syrup mixture (it will splatter) and stir. Sprinkle 1/2 cup nuts over bottom of cooled **Tart Shell**, then pour caramel over nuts. Chill until firm.

Place 1/2 cup cream into a saucepan and bring just to a boil. Add remaining 1 tablespoon butter, stir, then stir in chocolate chips. Mix thoroughly until chocolate melts. Pour over caramel layer, then chill until set.

Prepare **Cream Cheese Frosting** and spread on top of chilled chocolate layer, then chill again. If desired, combine 4 ounces melted chocolate with 2 to 3 tablespoons heavy cream and drizzle over tart. Sprinkle more chopped nuts around edge, if desired. Chill until ready to serve.

Because this dessert is prepared in steps, it isn't as difficult as it appears. And it's well worth the effort!

Serves 12

Tart Shell

1-1/4 cups all-purpose flour
2-1/2 tablespoons sugar
1/2 cup (1 stick) cold
   margarine, cut into small
   pieces
2 tablespoons ice water
1 large or 2 small egg yolks

In a food processor fitted with a steel blade, combine flour and sugar. Add butter and process until dough resembles coarse meal. Add ice water and egg yolks, and pulse just until dough will hold together (about 15 to 20 seconds). Form dough into a round, flat disk, wrap in plastic wrap, and chill for 30 minutes. (If desired, dough can be made ahead and chilled for a day or two, or frozen in advance.)

Roll out dough between 2 pieces of plastic wrap, place in a 9- or 10-inch tart pan, then cover and chill for 30 minutes. Meanwhile, preheat oven to 350 degrees. Prick crust well with a fork and bake until brown (about 20 minutes), then remove and set aside.

Makes 1 crust

Cream Cheese Frosting

1 (8-ounce) package cream
   cheese, room temperature
1/2 cup powdered sugar
1 tablespoon rum or brandy

In a small mixing bowl, beat together all ingredients until smooth.

Makes about 1 cup

THE ANAQUA GRILL
Plaza San Antonio Hotel
555 South Alamo Street
San Antonio, Texas 78205
(210) 229-1000

◙ Sawdust Pie

1-1/2 cups sugar
1-1/2 cups sweetened flaked
  coconut
1-1/2 cups chopped pecans
1-1/2 cups graham cracker
  crumbs
7 egg whites
1 teaspoon vanilla extract
1 (10-inch) unbaked pie shell
1 large banana, sliced thinly
Sweetened whipped cream
  and chopped pecans

Preheat oven to 350 degrees. In a large mixing bowl, combine sugar, coconut, pecans, graham cracker crumbs, egg whites, and vanilla. Stir until blended. Pour mixture into pie shell and bake for about 30 to 35 minutes. Cool to room temperature.

Arrange banana slices over top of pie, then cover with whipped cream and sprinkle with pecans. Refrigerate until ready to serve.

This special pie is Apple Annie's most requested and loved recipe.

Serves 8

APPLE ANNIE'S TEA ROOM & BAKERY
555 Bitters Road
San Antonio, Texas 78216
(210) 491-0226

◉ Zucchini Chocolate Cake

2-1/2 cups sugar
3-3/4 cups all-purpose flour
3/4 teaspoon baking powder
1-1/2 teaspoons baking soda
1/2 teaspoon ground cinnamon
1/2 cup cocoa
1/2 cup chopped walnuts
1/2 cup chocolate chips
1 cup buttermilk
1-1/2 cups vegetable oil
4 eggs
1/2 teaspoon vanilla extract
3 cups finely chopped zucchini
    (about 2 large)

Preheat oven to 350 degrees. In a large bowl, mix together sugar, flour, baking powder, baking soda, cinnamon, cocoa, walnuts, and chocolate chips. In a separate bowl, combine buttermilk, oil, eggs, vanilla, and zucchini.

Add wet mixture to dry ingredients and mix just until blended. Pour batter into a greased and floured Bundt pan. Bake for about 45 to 60 minutes, until a toothpick inserted in the center comes out clean. Cool cake in the pan for 15 minutes, then remove to a wire rack to finish cooling.

Zucchini adds extra moistness to this flavorful dessert, but otherwise can't be detected in the baked cake.

Serves 12 to 16

TWIN SISTERS BAKERY AND CAFE
6322 North New Braunfels
San Antonio, Texas 78209
(210) 822-2265

◉ Apple Annie's Carrot Cake with Cream Cheese–Raisin Frosting

2 cups all-purpose flour
2 cups sugar
1 teaspoon baking soda
1 teaspoon salt
2 teaspoons baking powder
2 teaspoons ground cinnamon
1 teaspoon vanilla extract
1 cup vegetable oil
4 large eggs
1/2 cup crushed pineapple, drained
1/2 cup sweetened flaked coconut
3 cups shredded carrots
1 cup pecans, chopped

Preheat oven to 350 degrees. Grease and flour a 9-by-13-inch baking pan (or two 8-inch round cake pans for a 2-layer cake; preheat oven to 325 degrees if using round cake pans).

In a large mixing bowl, combine flour, sugar, baking soda, salt, baking powder, and cinnamon. Add remaining ingredients in the order given (eggs 1 at a time), mixing well after each addition. Pour batter into prepared pan and bake for about 45 minutes (less time for smaller round pans) until a toothpick inserted in the center comes out clean. Prepare **Cream Cheese–Raisin Frosting** and spread over cooled cake (and between layers for 2-layer cake).

After serving, refrigerate any leftovers.

Serves 12

Cream Cheese–Raisin Frosting

1 (3-ounce) package cream cheese, room temperature
1/2 cup (1 stick) butter or margarine, room temperature
2-1/2 cups powdered sugar, sifted
1 teaspoon vanilla extract
1/2 cup raisins

In a mixing bowl, combine cream cheese and butter. Add powdered sugar and vanilla, and mix until creamy. Carefully stir in raisins.

APPLE ANNIE'S TEA ROOM & BAKERY
555 Bitters Road
San Antonio, Texas 78216
(210) 491-0226

◉ Chocolate Decadence Cheesecake

1-1/2 cups chocolate wafer
  crumbs
3–4 tablespoons butter, room
  temperature
3 (8-ounce) packages cream
  cheese, room temperature
1-1/4 cups sugar
1 teaspoon vanilla extract
3 tablespoons cake flour
4 eggs
4 (1-ounce) squares Baker's
  sweet chocolate, melted
1/4 cup evaporated milk

Thoroughly combine chocolate wafer crumbs and butter, and press onto bottom of a 9-inch springform pan. Refrigerate.

Preheat oven to 325 degrees. Using an electric mixer, whip cream cheese until fluffy. Gradually add sugar, then vanilla and flour. On low setting of mixer, add eggs, 1 at a time, followed by melted chocolate. Stir in milk.

Pour mixture into prepared crust and bake for 50 to 65 minutes. Allow cheesecake to set for 15 minutes before releasing sides of pan. Before releasing sides, go around edge of cheesecake with a sharp knife to loosen cake from edges. Let cool for at least 1 hour, then refrigerate until ready to serve.

This smooth and creamy chocolate cheesecake deserves its "decadent" name.

Serves 14 to 16

GREY MOSS INN
19010 Scenic Loop Road
Helotes, Texas 78023
(210) 695-8301

◉ The Peach Tree Cheesecake with Texas Praline Sauce

1-1/4 cups graham cracker
  crumbs
1/4 cup sugar
1/4 cup chopped walnuts or
  pecans
1/4 cup melted butter
4 (8-ounce) packages cream
  cheese, room temperature
1-1/2 cups firmly packed light
  brown sugar
3 tablespoons all-purpose flour
2-1/4 teaspoons vanilla extract
4 eggs
1 cup evaporated milk

Preheat oven to 325 degrees. Thoroughly combine graham cracker crumbs, sugar, nuts, and butter, and press onto bottom of a well-greased 9- or 10-inch springform pan. Bake for 15 minutes. Remove from oven and set aside.

Reduce oven temperature to 300 degrees. Using an electric mixer, beat softened cream cheese with brown sugar until well blended. Add flour, vanilla, and eggs (1 at a time), blending well after each addition. Gradually add evaporated milk. Scrape down sides of bowl frequently and remix until no lumps remain. Pour mixture into prepared crust and bake for 1 hour. Turn off heat and let cake cool in oven with door closed for several hours or overnight. Refrigerate cheesecake, then serve topped with warm **Texas Praline Sauce.**

The tea room has served this cheesecake since opening, and it continues to be the most popular one. If desired, you can omit the Texas Praline Sauce and serve the cake plain or with fresh fruit.

Serves 14 to 16

Texas Praline Sauce

1 cup firmly packed light
  brown sugar
2-1/2 tablespoons cornstarch
1-1/2 cups water
2 tablespoons butter or
  margarine
1/2 cup chopped pecans

In a small saucepan, combine brown sugar and cornstarch. Add water and cook, stirring constantly, over medium heat until thick and bubbly (about 5 minutes). Add butter and stir until melted. Stir in pecans and remove from heat.

This dark, rich sauce also can be used to top ice cream pie.

Makes about 2 cups

THE PEACH TREE GIFT GALLERY AND TEA ROOM
210 South Adams Street
Fredericksburg, Texas 78624
(210) 997-9527

◉ Breakfast Cheesecake

1 package yellow cake mix (not with pudding included)
1 cup large curd cottage cheese
2 (8-ounce) packages cream cheese, room temperature
1-1/2 teaspoons vanilla extract
1/2 cup sugar, plus 1/4 cup mixed with 1/2 teaspoon cinnamon
4 eggs

Preheat oven to 350 degrees. Prepare cake batter according to package directions and pour into a greased and floured 9-by-13-inch pan. In a large bowl, combine cottage cheese, cream cheese, vanilla, 1/2 cup sugar, and eggs, then pour over cake batter in prepared pan.

Bake for 30 minutes, then remove from oven and sprinkle top with sugar-cinnamon mixture. Return to oven and bake for 15 to 20 minutes more, or until the center no longer jiggles. (The cake and the cheese mixture trade places while baking.) Cool and slice to serve.

This cheesecake can be served as a breakfast goody or as a dessert with coffee in the evening. Though best eaten the same day it's prepared, it also freezes well.

Serves 12

SUGAR-BAKER'S
5114 Broadway
San Antonio, Texas 78209
(210) 820-0306

◉ Cajeta Crêpes

2 quarts whole milk
3 cups sugar
3/4 teaspoon baking soda
1-1/2 cups chopped pecans,
    plus additional to garnish
2 tablespoons butter
2 ounces brandy
8 crêpes

In a large stockpot, stir together milk, sugar, and baking soda to dissolve sugar. Bring to a boil over medium-high heat, then reduce heat and simmer, stirring occasionally, for 4 to 5 hours or until very thick and caramel colored. Refrigerate until ready to use.

Preheat oven to 350 degrees. Sauté pecans in butter in a skillet, then transfer to a baking sheet and toast until crisp (about 6 minutes; do not burn). Set aside.

When ready to serve, reheat about 1-1/2 cups of sauce in a large skillet along with toasted pecans and brandy. When sauce simmers, add 1 crêpe at a time, using tongs or 2 forks to fold crêpe in half and then in half again, forming a triangle. Transfer each finished crêpe to a dessert plate. Spoon additional sauce over each serving and garnish with pecans.

This sauce can be made up to 2 days before serving and stored in the refrigerator.

Serves 8

ERNESTO'S
2559 Jackson Keller
San Antonio, Texas 78230
(210) 344-1248

◉ Chocolate Banana Bread with Caramel Sauce

1/2 cup (1 stick) butter, room
 temperature
1 cup sugar
1/2 cup firmly packed brown
 sugar
2 eggs
4 ripe bananas, mashed
1 teaspoon baking soda
1/3 cup buttermilk
2 cups sifted flour
1 teaspoon ground cinnamon
1/2 teaspoon ground nutmeg
1 teaspoon salt
2 teaspoons vanilla extract
1 tablespoon cocoa
1 cup chopped roasted pecans,
 plus additional to garnish
1/2 cup raisins, chopped very
 fine
Vanilla ice cream

Preheat oven to 375 degrees. In a large bowl, cream together butter and sugars. Add eggs and beat well, then mix in bananas. Dissolve baking soda in buttermilk, then add to sugar mixture. Stir in remaining ingredients except ice cream and pour batter into 2 well-greased and floured loaf pans.

Bake until loaves test done when a toothpick is inserted into the center (about 40 to 45 minutes). Cool in pans for 20 minutes, then place on rack to finish cooling. To serve, place a warmed slice of bread in a pool of warm **Caramel Sauce.** Top bread with a scoop of ice cream, then sprinkle sauce with a few chopped nuts.

This delicious bread, which also can be enjoyed with bottled caramel sauce, heats well in the microwave and freezes well, too.

Makes 2 loaves

Caramel Sauce

1-1/2 cups sugar
1/4–1/2 cup water
2 cups heavy cream
1/2 cup (1 stick) butter

Place sugar in large heavy saucepan over medium high heat; do not stir. When sugar turns caramel colored, reduce heat and toss sugar to lightly brown all of it. When sugar turns to syrup, remove from heat and add water (the resulting mass of hard sugar will melt). Add cream and cook over low heat, stirring, until mixture thickens (about 10 minutes). Stir in butter until melted, then remove from heat and cool.

This sauce keeps well in the refrigerator. Reheat it in the top of a double boiler or in the microwave on low power.

Makes 3-1/2 cups

BOUDRO'S: A TEXAS BISTRO ON THE RIVER WALK
421 East Commerce Street
San Antonio, Texas 78205
(210) 224-8484

◎ Sugar-Baker's Crispy Sugar Cookies

2 cups (4 sticks) butter, room
    temperature
2-1/4 cups sugar
2 eggs, beaten
4 teaspoons vanilla extract
5 cups all-purpose flour
1 teaspoon baking soda
1 teaspoon cream of tartar

Using an electric mixer, cream together butter and 2 cups sugar. Add beaten eggs and vanilla. Sift together flour, soda, and cream of tartar, then slowly beat into butter mixture until well blended. Refrigerate dough in a covered container for at least 3 hours or overnight.

Preheat oven to 350 degrees. Roll chilled dough into 2-inch balls and coat each one thoroughly in remaining 1/4 cup sugar held in a small bowl. Place dough balls on a cookie sheet, then press flat with the bottom of a heavy glass dipped in sugar (to use an uncoated glass, place a piece of waxed paper between glass and dough ball to prevent sticking). Arrange on baking sheets and bake for about 12 to 15 minutes, or until golden. Let cookies cool for 1 minute on baking sheets, then remove to a wire rack to cool completely. Store in an airtight container.

These cookies stay crisp and delicious for several days. The dough can be kept in the refrigerator for up to a week before baking; just let it soften at room temperature for about 10 minutes before rolling into balls.

Makes 3 dozen

SUGAR-BAKER'S
5114 Broadway
San Antonio, Texas 78209
(210) 820-0306

◉ Extra-Crunchy Chocolate Chip Cookies

1 cup (2 sticks) margarine,
    room temperature
3/4 cup vegetable oil
1 cup sugar
1 cup firmly packed brown
    sugar
2 tablespoons milk
1 egg
2 teaspoons vanilla extract
3-1/2 cups all-purpose flour
2 teaspoons baking soda
1 cup uncooked oats
1 cup corn flakes or Rice Chex
    cereal
2 cups chocolate chips

Preheat oven to 350 degrees. Using an electric mixer, combine margarine, oil, sugars, and milk. Beat mixture until light and fluffy, then add egg and vanilla and beat for 1 to 2 minutes more. Add flour and baking soda and mix just enough to combine, then, stirring by hand, add oats, cereal, and chocolate chips. (Dough can be made ahead to this point and refrigerated for up to 2 days.) Drop dough by teaspoonsful onto ungreased baking sheets, and then bake for 12 minutes or until done.

This is a great cookie that is very crispy, even in humid areas. No one will ever guess what's in them, but they'll be back for more.

Makes 5 dozen

H-E-B MARKETPLACE
6501 Bandera Road
San Antonio, Texas 78238
(210) 647-2700

◉ Apple Annie's Sand Tarts

2 cups (4 sticks) butter, room
   temperature
4 cups all-purpose flour
1 cup powdered sugar, plus
   additional for rolling
1 cup chopped pecans
1 teaspoon vanilla extract

Preheat oven to 350 degrees. In a food processor or using an electric mixer, combine butter, flour, 1 cup powdered sugar, pecans, and vanilla just until mixed. Shape or roll dough into crescents or half moons, about 1 to 2 inches long. Place on ungreased baking sheets and bake for 10 to 13 minutes, or until lightly brown. Remove from baking sheets and, while warm, roll in powdered sugar.

These wonderful treats are sometimes called "Mexican wedding cookies." After a day, they can be rerolled in powdered sugar, if needed.

Makes 6 dozen

APPLE ANNIE'S TEA ROOM & BAKERY
555 Bitters Road
San Antonio, Texas 78216
(210) 491-0226

◎ Butterscotch Scotties

2 cups unsifted all-purpose
   flour
2 teaspoons baking powder
1 teaspoon baking soda
1 teaspoon salt
1 cup (2 sticks) butter, room
   temperature
1-1/2 cups firmly packed
   brown sugar
2 eggs
1 tablespoon water
1-1/2 cups uncooked oats
   (old-fashioned or instant)
1 (12-ounce) package
   butterscotch morsels
1/2 teaspoon orange extract

Combine flour, baking powder, soda, and salt in a medium bowl and set aside. In a large mixing bowl, beat together butter, sugar, eggs, and water until creamy. Gradually add flour mixture, then stir in oats, butterscotch morsels, and orange extract. Chill dough for about 30 minutes.

Preheat oven to 375 degrees. Spoon dough by rounded tablespoonsful onto greased baking sheets. Bake for 10 to 12 minutes, or until done.

This dough also can be shaped into a roll, wrapped in freezer paper, and frozen, to be sliced and baked as needed.

Makes 5 dozen

ARLENE'S CAFE
426 Seventh Street
Comfort, Texas 78013
(210) 995-3330

◉ Coconut Squares

3/4 cup (1-1/2 sticks) butter, room temperature

2-1/4 cups firmly packed brown sugar

1-1/2 cups unsifted all-purpose flour, plus 6 tablespoons sifted flour

4 eggs, slightly beaten

3/4 teaspoon salt

1-1/2 teaspoons vanilla extract

1-1/2 cups sweetened flaked coconut

1-1/2 cups chopped or sliced pecans

Preheat oven to 350 degrees. In a mixing bowl, cream butter and 3/4 cup brown sugar. Add unsifted flour and blend thoroughly. Spread dough into a well-greased 9-by-13-inch baking pan. Bake for 12 to 15 minutes, or until lightly brown (leave oven on after removing baked crust).

In another bowl, thoroughly combine eggs, salt, vanilla, coconut, pecans, sifted flour, and remaining 1-1/2 cups brown sugar. Spread over prepared crust, taking care not to break crust. Bake for 25 to 30 minutes, or until firm. Cut while warm into 2-inch squares.

The Comestible Shoppe's Maggie Sarno is famous for her delicious bars. These freeze and travel well.

Makes 2 dozen

THE COMESTIBLE SHOPPE
4611 McCullough
San Antonio, Texas 78212
(210) 824-4883

❂ Pecan Squares

3/4 cup (1-1/2 sticks) butter,
  room temperature
3/4 cup plus 1-1/2 tablespoons
  sugar
1 egg, separated
2-1/2 teaspoons ground
  cinnamon
1-1/2 cups all-purpose flour
2 cups coarsely chopped
  pecans

Preheat oven to 350 degrees. In a mixing bowl, cream butter and 3/4 cup sugar. Add egg yolk and beat well. Sift cinnamon with flour and mix into creamed mixture. Spread dough into a well-greased 9-by-13-inch baking pan.

In another bowl, beat egg white until frothy, then add remaining 1-1/2 tablespoons sugar. Spread mixture over dough, then, using fingertips, press pecans on top. Bake for 30 minutes, or until lightly brown. Cut while warm into 2-inch squares.

To make these tasty bars even prettier, cut the pecan halves crosswise instead of chopping them. These bars freeze well.

Makes 2 dozen

THE COMESTIBLE SHOPPE
4611 McCullough
San Antonio, Texas 78212
(210) 824-4883

◉ Mango Gelatin Molds

2 cups water
2 (3-ounce) packages lemon
  gelatin
1 (15-ounce) can mangoes with
  liquid
4 ounces (1/2 of an 8-ounce
  package) cream cheese,
  room temperature
Mint springs

In a saucepan, bring water to a boil, then stir in gelatin to dissolve. Let mixture cool slightly but not set.

In a blender or food processor, combine mangoes and juice with cream cheese, blending until mixture is smooth. Whisk blended mango mixture into dissolved gelatin, mixing well. Pour mixture into one 4-cup mold or eight 6-ounce molds. Chill for at least 4 hours. Unmold and garnish with mint sprigs.

This great summer dish can be served as a light dessert or as an accompaniment to other cold offerings, such as chicken salad.

Serves 8

CAPPY'S RESTAURANT
5011 Broadway
San Antonio, Texas 78209
(210) 828-9669

Restaurants

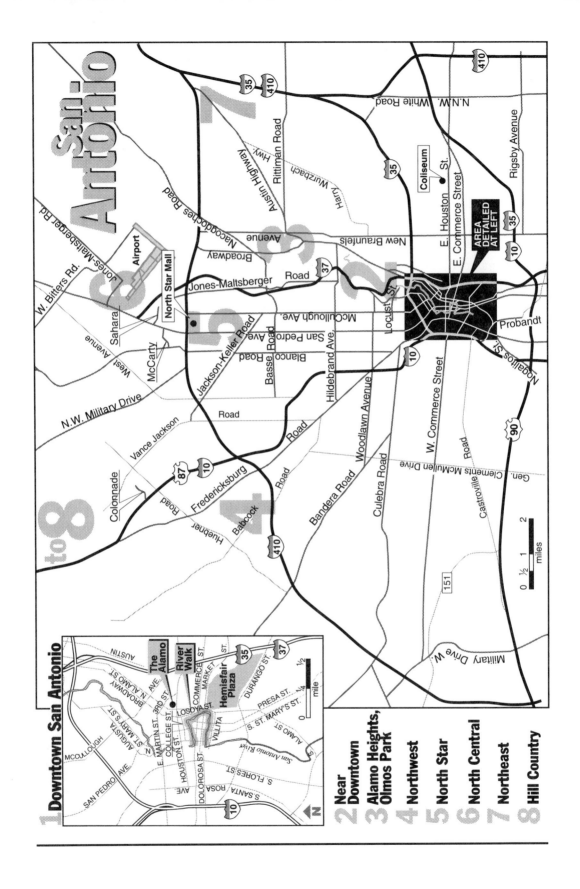

San Antonio

1 Downtown San Antonio
2 Near Downtown
3 Alamo Heights, Olmos Park
4 Northwest
5 North Star
6 North Central
7 Northeast
8 Hill Country

◪ Restaurant Listings

The following listings offer additional information about the restaurants represented in the recipe sections of this book.

KEY:
Prices/credit cards: $ (under $10); $$ ($10 to $20); $$$ ($20 and up); + (credit cards accepted); no + (credit cards not accepted)
Dress: C (casual); D (dressy)
Map locations: (1) Downtown; (2) Near Downtown; (3) Alamo Heights, Olmos Park; (4) Northwest; (5) North Star; (6) North Central; (7) Northeast; (8) Hill Country

Alamo Cafe, 9714 San Pedro, San Antonio, TX 78216, (210) 341-4526; 10060 Interstate 10 W., San Antonio, TX 78230, (210) 691-8827. Whether you're looking for fajitas, spicy enchiladas, tortilla soup, or chicken-fried steak, you'll find it at the Alamo Cafe. This restaurant was named one of Texas's top 10 by the readers of *Texas Highways.* $; +; C; (6), (4)

The Anaqua Grill, Plaza San Antonio Hotel, 555 S. Alamo St., San Antonio, TX 78205; (210) 229-1000. The Anaqua Grill offers innovative cosmopolitan dining in a lush garden setting. The eclectic cuisine features specials from the Mediterranean, the Pacific Rim, and the American Southwest, as well as Spanish-style tapas. $$; +; C; (1)

Apple Annie's Tea Room & Bakery, 555 Bitters Rd., San Antonio, TX 78216; (210) 491-0226. Located in Artisan's Alley amidst 22 specialty shops, the tea room offers old-fashioned favorites prepared fresh daily. Homemade soups, salads, sandwiches, and sinfully rich desserts are among the specialties. $; no +; C; (6)

Arlene's Cafe, 426 Seventh St., Comfort, TX 78013; (210) 995-3330. Located in a lovely Victorian home built in 1905, Arlene's is the next best thing to Grandma's house. Carefully prepared, artfully presented homemade soups, salads, breads, and desserts make this spot worth the drive from San Antonio. $; +; C; (8)

Barcelona's Mediterranean Cafe, 4901 Broadway, Ste. 120, San Antonio, TX 78209; (210) 822-6129. Specialties such as tapas and paella are among the top choices at this trendy, popular Alamo Heights restaurant. Try the daily specials with confidence. An interesting wine list is another draw. $$; +; C; (3)

Bistro Time, 5137 Fredericksburg Rd., San Antonio, TX 78229; (210) 344-6626. Bistro Time is a small chef/owner-operated restaurant that takes pride in offering freshly prepared American and continental cuisine served by a courteous, friendly staff. The wine menu is limited but selective and a good value. $$; +; C; (4)

Boardwalk Bistro, 4011 Broadway, San Antonio, TX 78209; (210) 824-0100. Nightly live entertainment and a large beer and wine selection add to the relaxed ambience at this comfortable, casual restaurant. An upscale vegetarian menu and a large appetizer list are among the restaurant's highlights. $$; +; C; (3)

Boccaccio Ristorante Italiano, 205 N. Presa St., San Antonio, TX 78205; (210) 225-1500. Located just one block off the River Walk, Boccaccio's offers a broad selection of Italian specialties in a comfortable atmosphere. Seafood is a highlight of the menu. $$; +; C; (1)

Boudro's: A Texas Bistro on the River Walk, 421 E. Commerce St., San Antonio, Texas 78205; (210) 224-8484. Boudro's is one of the most popular restaurants on the river. Enter from the street level on Commerce Street or from the River Walk. An eclectic menu combining the best of Cajun, Texas, and the Southwest offers something to please every diner. $$; +; C; (1)

Cactus Flower Cafe, Marriott Riverwalk, 711 E. Riverwalk, San Antonio, TX 78205; (210) 224-4555. House specialties here include a breakfast buffet, tortilla soup, fresh salads, prime rib, and fried ice cream. Outdoor dining overlooking the river is offered on Friday and Saturday evenings. $$; +; C; (1)

Cafe Camille, 517 E. Woodlawn, San Antonio, TX 78212; (210) 735-2307. Much like a side-street bistro in Paris, Cafe Camille walks a fine line between comfort and elegance and offers a unique and intimate dining experience. The menu and specials range from classical to innovative American entrees. $$; +; C; (2)

Cappy's Restaurant, 5011 Broadway, San Antonio, TX 78209; (210) 828-9669. This restaurant is an Alamo Heights tradition. Known for its unique eclectic Texas cuisine, Cappy's offers indoor dining on two levels, or outdoors on a beautiful patio. The kitchen staff will accommodate the needs of customers on special diets. $$; +; C; (3)

Carranza Grocery & Market, 701 Austin St., San Antonio, TX 78215; (210) 223-0903. Four generations of the Carranza family operate this popular restaurant, located in a historic limestone building built around 1870. The eclectic menu features barbecue and Mexican specialties as well as seafood, steaks, and Italian cuisine. $$; +; C/D; (1)

Cascabel Restaurant, Sheraton Fiesta Hotel, 37 N.E. Loop 410, San Antonio, TX 78216; (210) 366-2424. A special selection of chilies, cacti, and regional ingredients add spice to Cascabel's menu, which features the cuisine of the Texas Southwest combined with authentic cooking techniques of Mexico. $$$; +; C; (6)

Chaps Restaurant/River Bend Saloon, Hyatt Regency San Antonio, 123 Losoya, San Antonio, TX 78205; (210) 222-1234. Chaps, with a casual Southwestern atmosphere, specializes in a made-to-order pasta bar. River Bend Saloon on the River Walk has a country-western atmosphere and specializes in barbecue brisket, chicken, and prime rib smoked on the premises. $; +; C; (1)

The Colonial Room Restaurant, The Menger Hotel, 204 Alamo Plaza, San Antonio, TX 78205; (210) 223-4361. The Colonial Room Restaurant has been in continuous operation for more than a century. The menu includes popular historical recipes as well as contemporary Southwest favorites. Don't miss the mango ice cream and tortilla soup here. $$; +; C; (1)

The Comestible Shoppe, 4611 McCullough, San Antonio, TX 78212; (210) 824-4883. The Comestible Shoppe is San Antonio's original gourmet carryout. This distinguished food boutique offers everything from a simple sandwich to special holiday dinners. Leave room for owner Maggie Sarno's famous desserts. $; +; C; (3)

The Copper Kitchen, The Southwest Craft Center, 300 Augusta St., San Antonio, TX 78205; (210) 224-0123. The original dining area for the residents of the Old Ursuline Academy is now the Copper Kitchen, a luncheon restaurant serving a delicious home-style menu at reasonable prices. Choose from sandwiches, salads, and two hot entrees that change daily. $; no +; C; (1)

The Courtyard at La Lou, 2632 Broadway, San Antonio, TX 78212; (210) 225-7987. Located adjacent to its sister restaurant, La Louisiane, The Courtyard features patio dining and a French Creole menu. The Courtyard also offers a late-night menu, specialty desserts, and exotic coffees. $$; +; C; (2)

Crosswalk Deli, 121-C Alamo Plaza, San Antonio, TX 78205; (210) 228-0880. A casual sidewalk cafe with a view of Alamo Plaza, the Crosswalk Deli is downtown's healthy choice. Continental breakfast is served until 11 a.m.; lunch features a variety of soups, salads, sandwiches, and cookies. $; no +; C; (1)

Crumpets, 5800 Broadway, Ste. 302, San Antonio, TX 78209; (210) 821-5600. Chef/owner François Maeder offers traditional continental cuisine—fish, fowl and steak with exceptional sauces—as well as lighter fare, such as pasta and heart-healthy dishes. $$; +; C/D; (3)

El Mirador Restaurant, 722 S. St. Mary's St., San Antonio, TX 78205; (210) 225-9444. Owners Julian, Maria, and Diana Trevino are in charge of this casual restaurant famous as a San Antonio tradition. Known for its Mexican soups (which have been written about in *The New York Times*), El Mirador also offers a more upscale dinner menu. $; +; C; (1)

Ernesto's, 2559 Jackson Keller, San Antonio, TX 78230; (210) 344-1248. Tortilla soup, crabmeat and shrimp nachos, Crab and Shrimp Crêpes Veracruz, and Crab Mexicana are among the specialties at this delightful restaurant. Gourmet awards include one for the best green salsa in San Antonio. $$; +; C; (4)

Fiesta Texas Catering, 17000 Interstate 10 W., San Antonio, TX 78269; (210) 697-5164. Fiesta Texas may be best known for its live entertainment and thrilling rides, but the catering department of the theme park prides itself on the ability to create a wide variety of events ranging from company picnics to intimate dinners for two. $$; +; C/D; (8)

Fig Tree Restaurant, 515 Paseo De La Villita, San Antonio, TX 78205; (210) 224-1976. Located in historic La Villita overlooking the River Walk, the Fig Tree offers beef Wellington, chateaubriand, quail, and fresh salmon among its long-standing specialties. Elegant linens, Gorham crystal, Pickard china, and crystal knife rests grace the tables. $$$; +; D; (1)

410 Diner, 8315 Broadway, San Antonio, TX 78209; (210) 822-6246. Home-style cooking Texas-style is the highlight of this diner. An assortment of freshly cooked vegetables, including skin-on mashed potatoes, accompany entrees such as meatloaf, chicken-fried steak, and grilled chicken. $; +, C; (3)

Gini's Home Cooking & Bakery, 7214 Blanco Rd., San Antonio, TX 78216; (210) 342-2768. Gini's wide-ranging menu offers everything from country-fried steak and pork chops to Pritikin spaghetti. Vegetarian dishes are given star treatment here. Non-smoking restaurant since 1982. $; +; C; (6)

Grey Moss Inn, 19010 Scenic Loop Rd., Helotes, TX 78023; (210) 695-8301. Located on the historic Scenic Loop northwest of San Antonio, the restaurant here offers Southern hospitality and fine food in a romantic setting. Founded in 1929, the inn is known for its steaks and cumin-herbed squash casserole. $$$; +; C/D; (8)

H-E-B Marketplace, 6501 Bandera Rd., San Antonio, TX 78238; (210) 647-2700. H-E-B grocery stores are a Texas tradition started in the Texas Hill Country town of Kerrville in 1904. Recently H-E-B has started doing the cooking for busy shoppers, offering prepared foods in the upscale setting of H-E-B Marketplace. $; no +; C; (4)

La Calesa, 2103 E. Hildebrand, San Antonio, TX 78209; (210) 822-4475. Since 1983 La Calesa has been cooking with the authentic herbs, spices, and ingredients typical of the Yucatán. The guacamole is memorable. This restaurant has been critically acclaimed by *Texas Monthly, Travel Holiday,* and the *San Antonio Express-News.* $$; +; C; (3)

La Madeleine French Bakery & Cafe, 4820 Broadway, San Antonio, TX 78209; (210) 829-7279. Enjoy a casual French country atmosphere and authentic French breads, pastries, soups, salads, pastas, rotisserie chicken, and more at La Madeleine. Fat-free, preservative-free breads baked in a wood-burning oven are a highlight. $; +; C; (3)

Las Canarias, La Mansion del Rio Hotel, 112 College St., San Antonio, TX 78205; (210) 225-2581. Among the highlights at Las Canarias is the bounteous Sunday brunch, complete with seafood and sushi stations, known as one of the best in the city. Southwestern-inspired entrees are also a favorite. $$$; +; C/D; (1)

L'Etoile, 6106 Broadway, San Antonio, TX 78209; (210) 826-4551. Tucked away in fashionable Alamo Heights just minutes from downtown and the Loop is L'Etoile, a French restaurant of merit. Traditional French cuisine is offered in a comfortable, tasteful atmosphere. Order lobster with confidence. $$$; +; C, (3)

Luigi's Restaurant, 6825 San Pedro, San Antonio, TX 78216; (210) 349-5251. Luigi Ciccarelli, owner of Luigi's, operates one of the more established Italian restaurants in the city. Saltimbocca alla Luigi and cold spinach salad are among the restaurant's favorites. $$; +; C; (2)

Morton's of Chicago, The Steakhouse, 849 E. Commerce St., San Antonio, TX 78205; (210) 228-0700. Morton's of Chicago has made a name for itself in San Antonio. This clubby, yet sophisticated, restaurant specializes in USDA prime, aged steaks, including the signature 24-ounce Porterhouse and a 20-ounce New York strip. $$$; +; C/D; (1)

New Braunfels Smokehouse, 6450 N. New Braunfels, San Antonio, TX 78209, (210) 826-6008; 140 Hwy. 46 S., New Braunfels, TX 78130, (210) 625-2416. Established almost half a century ago in nearby New Braunfels, this smokehouse has become a Hill Country, and now a San Antonio, tradition. Enjoy famous hickory-smoked meats at the restaurant or have them shipped nationwide. $; +; C; (3), (8)

Old San Francisco Steak & Seafood House, 10223 Sahara, San Antonio, TX 78216; (210) 342-2321. Recognized the world over for its unique atmosphere, and consistently awarded the American Angus Association Award of Excellence, this Gay '90s Barbary Coast–style steak house offers a menu rich with choices from steaks and prime rib to seafood and pasta. $$$; +; C/D; (6)

The Olive Garden Italian Restaurant, 849 E. Commerce St., San Antonio, TX 78205, (210) 224-5956; 7920 Interstate 35 N., San Antonio, TX 78218, (210) 650-5883; 6155 N.W. Loop 410, San Antonio, TX 78201, (210) 520-7935; 13730 San Pedro, San Antonio, TX 78232, (210) 494-3411. Famous for its salad, warm garlic breadsticks, and fresh pasta, The Olive Garden offers an extensive menu of Northern- and Southern-style Italian specialties. Seasonal specialties also are offered. $; +; C; (1), (7), (4), (6)

The Original Mexican Restaurant, 528 River Walk, San Antonio, TX 78205; (210) 224-9951. The 1988 Original Mexican Restaurant pays tribute to the 1899 Original Mexican Restaurant that overlooked the river from Losoya Street. The new Original offers mango margaritas, sizzling fajitas, and other Mexican dishes in a River Walk or dining room setting. $; +, C; (1)

Paesano's, 1715 McCullough, San Antonio, TX 78212; (210) 226-9541. For approximately 25 years Paesano's has been a San Antonio landmark, known as a great place to eat and see and be seen. Try old favorites such as Shrimp Paesano or branch out into owner Joe Cosniac's new, more healthful low-fat specialties. $$; +; C; (2)

The Peach Tree Gift Gallery and Tea Room, 210 S. Adams St., Fredericksburg, TX 78624; (210) 997-9527. Located approximately an hour from San Antonio in the Texas Hill Country, The Peach Tree Tea Room is a wonderful place to enjoy such specialties as soups, salads, sandwiches, and lush desserts while browsing through lovely gift items. $; +; C; (8)

Polo's at the Fairmount, 401 S. Alamo St., San Antonio, TX 78205; (210) 224-8800. Located in the historic Fairmount Hotel, which is listed in the *Guinness Book of World Records* as the largest building ever moved, Polo's offers American cuisine and pizzas prepared in a wood-burning oven. The bar is a good place to visit with friends and watch the activity on South Alamo Street. $$$; +; C/D; (1)

Pour la France, 7959 Broadway, San Antonio, TX 78209; (210) 826-4333. This casual bistro offers a variety of soup, salad, and sandwich favorites as well as French-style pizzas and a bounteous array of baked goods. This is a good choice for a casual light or filling breakfast as well. $$; +; C; (3)

Restaurant Biga, 206 E. Locust St., San Antonio, TX 78212; (210) 225-0722. Nationally recognized chef Bruce Auden's menu changes daily, depending on what's freshest and in season. Order game and seafood specialties with confidence; be sure to leave room for Biga's desserts. The attached LocuStreet Bakery offers wonderful European-style breads. $$; +; C; (2)

Ruffino's Restaurant & Bar, 9802 Colonnade, San Antonio, TX 78230; (210) 641-6100. Shrimp Ruffino's, Ruffino's Special Salad, and dessert soufflés are among the house specialties here. Enjoy the Italian/continental menu while listening to live music. Dancing available nightly. $$; +; C; (4)

Ruth's Chris Steak House, 7720 Jones-Maltsberger, Ste. 118, San Antonio, TX 78216; (210) 821-5051. U.S. prime beef served on sizzling platters is the specialty of the house here. Traditional Creole favorites such as shrimp remoulade, shrimp cocktail, and bread pudding with whiskey sauce are also offered in this restaurant's turn-of-the-century eclectic setting. $$$; +; C/D; (5)

Stetson Restaurant, Hilton Palacio del Rio Hotel, 200 S. Alamo St., San Antonio, TX 78205; (210) 222-1400. The Stetson's specialties, such as Southwestern ravioli, mesquite-grilled lamb chops, and Shrimp Cancún, combined with a spectacular view of the River Walk, offers downtown diners an exquisite dinner experience. $$; +; C/D; (1)

Sugar-Baker's, 5114 Broadway, San Antonio, TX 78209; (210) 820-0306. Sugar-Baker's is a neighborhood deli, bakery, and sweet shop located in downtown Alamo Heights—an ideal spot to grab a quick bite to eat. Or, pick up some gourmet candies and chocolates or freshly baked cookies to go—bagged or in gift baskets or tins. $; no +; C; (3)

Teka Molino, 7231 San Pedro, San Antonio, TX 78216, (210) 344-7281; 2403 N. St. Mary's St., San Antonio, TX 78212, (210) 735-5471. Teka Molino has been in operation for approximately 50 years, serving up such specialties as puffy tacos, bean rolls, and enchiladas. Nightly specials are a delight, as are the restaurant's tortilla soup and *caldo.* Closed weekends. $; no +; C; (2), (5)

Thai Kitchen, 445 McCarty, San Antonio, TX 78216; (210) 344-8366. Thai Kitchen is one of San Antonio's most popular ethnic restaurants. Exquisite appetizers, soups, and curries are menu favorites, but whatever you order, be sure to save room for the restaurant's signature dessert, Coconut Sorbet. $; +; C; (6)

Tower of the Americas, 222 Hemisfair Plaza, San Antonio, TX 78210; (210) 223-3101. Get a bird's-eye view of downtown San Antonio and the surrounding area in this revolving restaurant on the site of the 1968 World's Fair. Prime rib and seafood are among the restaurant's specialties. $$; +; C; (1)

Twin Sisters Bakery and Cafe, 6322 N. New Braunfels, San Antonio, TX 78209; (210) 822-2265. Twin Sisters' health-conscious menu includes a selection of vegetarian and nonvegetarian dishes prepared daily from the freshest ingredients. A variety of chef's specials are also available, as well as an array of fresh baked goods. $; no +; C; (3)

Villa Italian Specialties, 910 North Star Mall, San Antonio, TX 78216; (210) 342-3428. This casual restaurant, located in the picnic court of North Star Mall, is the perfect place to grab an Italian specialty while taking a break from shopping at San Antonio's largest shopping area. $; no +; C; (5)

Water Street Oyster Bar, 999 E. Basse, Ste. 130, San Antonio, TX 78209; (210) 829-4853. This Alamo Heights eatery offers a variety of daily specials sure to please seafood lovers. A casual, comfortable atmosphere offers pleasant surroundings to enjoy the restaurant's signature Caldo Xochitl and praline cheesecake. $$; +; C; (3)

Zuni Grill, 511 E. Riverwalk, San Antonio, TX 78205; (210) 227-0864. Start with cactus pear margaritas, then move on to such specialties as Venison Medallions with Chimichurri Relish and Grilled Shrimp and Chicken Anticuchos. This is a great place to enjoy breakfast and a view of the River Walk. $$; +; C; (1)

⚥ Restaurant Index

◪ Recipe Index

The bold asterisk (*) preceding a recipe title indicates a "recipe within a recipe"; that is, one that appears within the preparation instructions for a primary recipe, but which in some cases could stand alone or be served with another favorite dish.

BEGINNINGS

MAIN COURSES

SWEET ENDINGS

◪ About the Author

Karen Haram began working for the *San Antonio Express-News* as food writer in 1980 and was named food editor in 1985. She was a contributing editor for *Cook's* magazine and a restaurant reviewer for *San Antonio Monthly* magazine, as well as food writer for the *Lubbock Avalanche-Journal* and the *Kankakee Daily Journal.* She has won more than 75 awards for her newspaper work.

Karen is as comfortable working in her own kitchen as she is dining out. Her love of good food began in southern Illinois, where growing up on a farm taught her the joys of cooking and eating fresh foods, and it was honed during moves to central and upstate Illinois, west and south Texas, Georgia, Alabama, and Okinawa. She is an avid cooking-class fan and has taken classes in the United States, Asia, and Europe.

A contributing editor for *Texas the Beautiful* cookbook, Karen is secretary of the Association of Food Journalists, an organization for which she also served as regional codirector. She is on the council of the Texas Hill Country Wine and Food Festival and has served as a judge for the James Beard Food and Beverage Book Awards, the R.T. French Tastemaker Awards, and the Bert Greene Food Writing Contest.

She was on the planning committee of the 1993 Newspaper Food Editors and Writers Association convention and is assistant general chairman of the 1995 International Association of Culinary Professionals convention. She is a member of Texas Press Women, the National Federation of Press Women, and a board member and secretary of the James Madison High School Spirit Club. She was the Texas Press Women District 7 nominee for Communicator of Achievement for Texas in 1994.

In addition to serving as a celebrity judge for the March of Dimes Gourmet Gala, Karen has judged the National Beef Cook-Off, the Texas Beef Cook-Off, and the World's Championship Chili Cook-Off, as well as dozens of culinary competitions (including a *menudo* contest) on the local and state level.

Karen and her husband Mark have two daughters, Jennifer and Emily. In her spare time, Karen enjoys cooking, entertaining, reading, antiquing, and needle-pointing.